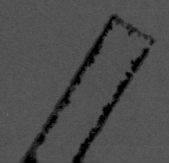

FAITH HAS NEED
OF ALL THE TRUTH

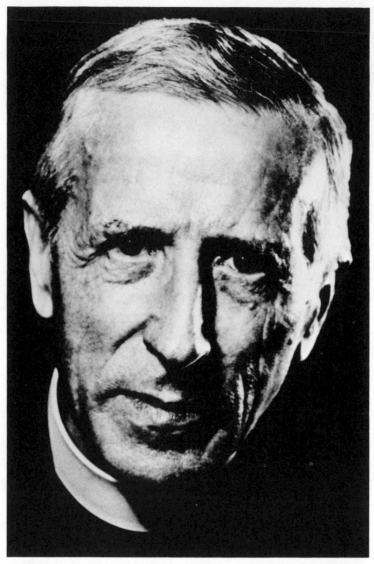

Pierre Teilhard de Chardin in 1955, photographed by Philippe Halsman, courtesy Wide World Photos

FAITH HAS NEED OF ALL THE TRUTH

A Life of Pierre Teilhard de Chardin

by CHARLIE MAY SIMON

E. P. Dutton & Co., Inc. New York

Library of Congress Cataloging in Publication Data

Simon, Charlie May (Hogue)
Faith has need of all the truth.

SUMMARY: Biography of the paleontologist, priest, writer,
and co-discoverer of Peking man who developed a theory
claiming to unify cosmic evolution and Christianity.

1. Teilhard de Chardin, Pierre—Juvenile literature.
[1. Teilhard de Chardin, Pierre.   2. Scientists.
3. Philosophers]   I. Title.

B2430.T374S53   194[B]   [92]   73–16303
ISBN 0–525–29606–9

Published simultaneously in Canada by Clarke,
Irwin & Company Limited, Toronto and Vancouver

Designed by Riki Levinson
Printed in the U.S.A.
First Edition

Acknowledgments

Permission to reprint the following copyrighted material is gratefully acknowledged:

To Harper & Row for selections from the following works by Pierre Teilhard de Chardin: *The Future of Man*, 1964; *Hymn of the Universe*, 1965; *Letters from a Traveler*, 1962; *The Phenomenon of Man*, 1969; and from *The Teilhard de Chardin Album*, 1966, edited by Jeanne Mortier and Marie-Louise Auboux.

To The New Seabury Press for *In the Field with Teilhard de Chardin* by George B. Barbour, © 1965 by Herder & Herder, Inc.

To Lois and Neil Park

Contents

1
Auvergne

THE DARK, TORMENTED HILLS of the French province of
Auvergne had risen in violence out of a spewing mass of
fire, gas, and molten rock. The eruption occurred suddenly
and so long ago that there were no human eyes to witness
it. But hundreds of thousands of years have gone into
molding their shapes: the gnarled and twisted pinnacles,
like pointing fingers piercing the low-moving clouds, the
domed hills, some wooded and some as barren as the moon,
and the chalice-like craters filled with clear blue water.
Surrounding Auvergne's fertile plains, the hills appear
solid and imperturbable. Yet they are still in a never-
ending process of change, slowly contracting and expand-
ing with the rhythm of cold and heat, worn by rain, snow,
and icy winds, and sliced by swift-flowing streams.

Strangers coming to this part of France call it austere

and forbidding, but no one is more loyal to his land than the native of Auvergne. He loves it in all its moods, from its savage winter, when the mountain passes are hidden by snow and the wind cuts like a knife, to the gentle days of midsummer.

Emmanuel Teilhard de Chardin, a gentleman-farmer and owner of several estates in the region around Clermont-Ferrand, was a true son of Auvergne. He was a scholarly man and had made a study of old archives, tracing the history of the province from the time the Romans built a temple to Mercury on the summit of the nearby Puy du Dôme, through the devastations of the Normans and Visigoths, on to the first Crusade, which started from Clermont in 1096. He was interested not only in Auvergne's past, but in the land itself: the wild life, the plants, both rare and familiar, the many species of quartz found among the lava. He instilled in his children this knowledge and love of the land so that all became ardent naturalists. To one especially, his fourth child, Pierre, it became an absorbing passion that lasted throughout his life.

In 1875 Emmanuel Teilhard de Chardin married Berthe-Adèle de Dompierre d'Hornoy and brought her to Auvergne from her native Picardy. She was delicately beautiful, and though the great-grandniece of that irascible nonbeliever Voltaire, she was deeply pious. Eleven children were born to the marriage. They were an affectionate family, and each new baby was lovingly welcomed.

Pierre, christened Marie-Joseph Pierre, was born May 1, 1881, at Sarcenat, one of the family's three palatial homes. There was an older brother, Albéric, and a sister, Françoise. Another brother had died in infancy. Pierre was a year old when his sister Marguerite-Marie, affectionately called Guiguite, was born. After her there were Gabriel,

Olivier, Joseph, Louise, called Lou Lou, Gonzague, and Victor.

With so many brothers and sisters, fairly close in age, and as many cousins, the children had little need for outside companionship. They spent the severest months of winter, from January to March, in Clermont-Ferrand, at the townhouse Fontfreyde, which their father had inherited jointly with a cousin, Cirice Teillard de Chambon, who had given his name a different spelling. He and his wife were always called Uncle Cirice and Aunt Marie by the Teilhard de Chardin children, and their five children were more like brothers and sisters than distant cousins.

The house was old, dating back to the time of the Crusades. When the snow lay deep and the winter wind howled against the windowpanes, the cold and dampness of all the past centuries seemed trapped and held within its walls. Like all the old houses of Clermont, including the domed cathedral, Fontfreyde was built of the black lava of the region. It was somber in appearance inside as well as out, with many high-ceilinged rooms, long shadowy halls, and wide stairways. But a house so filled with children was anything but gloomy. When the weather kept them from ice-skating or coasting down snow-crusted slopes, they played indoors. Protected against the cold by woolen clothes, black-ribbed stockings over long underwear, and high-laced shoes, they raced from room to room and up and down the halls.

"That terrible quartet!" their cousin Marguerite said of Albéric, Pierre, and two younger brothers. In boisterous moods they teased the sedate little girls. They banged on doors and shouted war cries. The girls' long braids were pulled, which brought tears of protest. But when a maid came in bringing a tray of cakes and jam and oranges, peace was restored.

With the coming of spring the two families left for their separate country estates, but they frequently exchanged visits. The Teilhard de Chardins went first to Murol, on the banks of the Allier River, where they stayed until after Easter. They came again in autumn for a few weeks of hunting and fishing. The rest of the year was spent at Sarcenat, outside the village of Orcines. This was the place they would always look upon as home.

The house, white-plastered with gray shutters beside the long, narrow windows, was not as magnificent as the manor house of Murol. It was huge, rambling, with an uneven roof line and a bell-shaped tower that seemed to have been added as an afterthought.

Sarcenat had been in the family since 1820. Beneath one of the windows there still remained a stone carving of three roses, the coat of arms of the former owners. The Teilhard de Chardins' family coat of arms was two dragons upholding a crown, surrounded by words from Virgil: "Fiery is their vigor, and of heaven their source."

Life was relaxed and carefree for the Teilhard children, yet it was not without a certain discipline. Their days followed a set pattern. By half past seven in the morning they were up and having breakfast with the governess in her room. Lessons followed, with a pause for lunch at eleven. Both parents supervised their education. Their mother taught them their first lessons in reading and writing, and she heard their daily recitation of the catechism. Their father selected the books they were given to read, and he conducted the Latin lessons himself until the children were ready for secondary school. Tall, erect, with an aristocratic bearing, he had the air of one accustomed to respect. Yet his children knew him as a tender, devoted father.

He pointed out the stars to them and taught them the

names of the planets, and he showed them how to follow the course of the clouds. On their walks about the country-side he encouraged them to make collections of the things they were interested in. They brought home wild flowers to be pressed, butterflies, and various kinds of insects. These they learned to classify, label, and mount in glass cases. For his collection Pierre chose beetles, hard-backed and horny, instead of the fragile butterflies and flowers. From his early childhood he found comfort in things of substance, things that were firm and durable.

One evening when he was about five, he sat on a stool beside the hearth fire while his mother trimmed his curls. The blue flame, flickering over the logs, fascinated him. It seemed so pure and intangible, yet so real. Impulsively he picked up one of the curls and held it before the fire. He dropped it from his hand and it disappeared in flames. Nothing was left of what had so recently been a part of him. For the first time he had a feeling of insecurity, a knowledge that he was perishable.

Later he found a discarded iron plowshare, a treasure that he cherished above all the things in his collection. He kept it in a secret place in the corner of the courtyard. There it took on a personality of its own for him, some-thing harder, tougher, more lasting than anything in the world. But there came a time when he found that it had rusted, and he realized that even iron was impermanent. Again he felt the despair of a sensitive child. He threw himself on the lawn and shed bitter tears. It may have been pointed out to him by sympathetic parents that the molten rock from which iron was extracted was a far more durable substance, for from then on his interest turned to stones. He started a collection of the most glittering, trans-lucent, beautifully colored ones he could find.

Every evening after supper the family and the household servants gathered in the dining room for prayers. Pierre had his own favorite place to pray, kneeling beside the wall a little apart from the others. The children grew and developed under the influence of their mother's devotion to religion. High-spirited and happy though they were, they were also pious. "My dear sainted Maman. I owe to her all that is best in my soul," Pierre would say of her many years after.

On a wall in the drawing room at Sarcenat hung a picture representing Christ offering His heart to the world. From the window of the same room one looked out on a vista of volcanic hills. These two, the Sacred Heart and the firm earth, molded Pierre and set the pattern his life would follow.

It was the custom in the family, after the children had completed their elementary education at home, to send the sons to a Jesuit secondary school and the daughters to a school in Clermont run by the Ursuline nuns. Pierre was eleven when he was enrolled at Notre Dame de Mongré, where Albéric had gone before him. In April, soon after the opening of school, Pierre made his first communion. Then classes began, with lectures and study periods.

The school was at Villefranche, in the neighboring province of Beaujolais, but to a boy away from his family for the first time, it seemed far away. He had been so well taught at home that he had no trouble with his studies. But there were no lessons in geology, and he missed the walks with his father and his search for unusual stones. Three months after entering the school he was already thinking of the coming August vacation. "Even if my passion for stones, and even more for antiquities, has not completely flared up again, I shall rekindle it during the summer holidays, for the fire is in me, more active than ever," he wrote his parents.

One of his teachers at Mongré, Henri Bremond, would later recall a certain third-year pupil from Auvergne, "very intelligent, first in every subject, but disconcertingly sophisticated. Even the most restive or dull-witted boys sometimes took a real interest in their work; a more lively lesson or a more exciting assignment brought a light to their eyes. Not so this boy: and it was only long afterwards that I learned the secret of his seeming indifference. Transporting his mind far away from us was another, a jealous and absorbing passion—rocks."

Pierre's grades were outstanding in languages and science, but not in religious subjects. It was not that he lacked religious feeling, but the lessons were boring, with dry-as-dust textbooks that had remained unchanged for centuries. In his third year Pierre made his act of consecration to the Blessed Virgin, and he took an active part in the sodalities, religious groups of boys the same age. He was elected secretary of his sodality, and later president. The boys were encouraged to visit the hospital and the home for aged men, to cheer the patients with small gifts and music. "I wish Guiguite would send me a little red retreat-notebook that's in the desk of the yellow room, and also a little prayer that's in her prayers of St. Gertrude," Pierre wrote in one of his letters home. He was especially impressed by a remark made by one of his philosophy teachers, that holiness could be attained by simple virtues and the performance of everyday duties, as well as by martyrdom and miracles.

In his fifth and last year of school, Pierre and his classmates were photographed together. Dressed alike in light trousers and dark coat, stiff white collar and black tie, the other boys struck self-conscious poses. Pierre alone seemed unaware of the camera. His eyes were turned away in a serious, thoughtful expression. He was sixteen then, and facing an important decision in his life. He wanted to become a priest. The school motto was "God's Will Is My Will." A question kept coming to his mind: Was this God's will as well as his own? He must be sure before he took the step. A few weeks before the end of school he wrote to his parents.

"I must tell you first of all that nothing is completely decided. At the same time (and those I've consulted agree with me) it does seem to me as though God is offering me a vocation to leave the world. You can well imagine that once I am certain that I'm not mistaken, I shall answer the call; and I know, too, that you will be the last to raise any difficulties. All I need now is for our Lord to make me feel unmistakably what he wants of me and to give me the generosity of spirit that is needed."

As he supposed, his parents made no objection to his decision, but when he returned home they found him so thin and run-down that his father urged him to wait until he had regained his strength. He remained with his family for over a year. His weekdays were spent studying under a private tutor for his baccalaureate in mathematics, and on Sundays he was off in search of stones and minerals. He would always look back upon this last long period at Sarcenat and Clermont, sure that greater happiness was not to be found on earth.

He successfully passed his baccalaureate in May 1898, before a local jury in Clermont. The following year, six weeks before his eighteenth birthday, he left for the Jesuit novitiate at Aix-en-Provence.

II
Jesuit Novice

PIERRE TEILHARD began his preparation for the priesthood
with a retreat of thirty days in solitary meditation and self-
examination, and in contemplating the *Spiritual Exercises*
of St. Ignatius, founder of the Society of Jesus. He had
fifteen years of training before him, and the most exacting
would be the first two years as a novice. It was a period of
probation to test his fitness for the vocation.

"Man is created to praise, reverence, and serve God our
Lord, and so doing save his soul," Ignatius had written in
the *Exercises,* intended originally as a guide for his own
spiritual development. "Up to my sixth and twentieth year
I was entirely given to the vanities of the world," he said in
his latter years. "Above all I found pleasure in the man-
agement of arms and felt a keen and empty craving to
excel."

As a proud Spanish nobleman Ignatius had known no other life than that of courtier and soldier until 1521, when he was wounded in a battle against the French. He was brought to his father's ancestral castle in northern Spain with one leg badly shattered. The bones, which had been clumsily set, had to be broken and set again. In the solitude of a slow and painful convalescence, Ignatius was profoundly moved by a book on the lives of the saints. After great inner struggle he decided—a decision that was to have its effect throughout the world and for centuries to come—that from then on he would fight a different kind of battle: he would be a soldier of Christ.

As soon as his strength returned, Ignatius, then the young knight Iñigo of Loyola, bade his parents farewell and set out by muleback on a pilgrimage to the Benedictine Abbey of Montserrat in northeast Spain. On the way he changed from his luxurious clothes, wearing instead a garment of sackcloth and hempen shoes, and carried the gourd, bread sack, and staff of a mendicant. He remained for three days at the Abbey, where he made a confession of all his past. Before leaving he kept an all-night vigil before the altar of the Virgin, then placed on it his sword and dagger, symbols of his vanity. He left his mule to the Abbey and gave to a beggar the rich clothes he had worn from his father's castle.

He made his way on foot to the town of Manresa, close to Barcelona, where he lived for a year, spending much of the time in a damp cave beneath a cliff. There he fasted and spent long hours in prayer and meditation. And there, too, he began the book of instructions to himself that he called *Spiritual Exercises*.

"If I desire to awaken in me heartfelt sorrow for the sufferings of Christ, then I must suffer no pleasant thoughts, however good and holy, to enter in, but I must rouse myself to sorrow, grief, and pain by calling to mind the griefs, pains, and sorrows of our Lord from His birth to His passion."

Under the guidance of an understanding director, the young novices at Aix-en-Provence, each alone in a cell as dark as the cave of Manresa, knelt or sat in a certain way, breathing in and out according to the instructions as they prayed or meditated. They read passages of the *Spiritual Exercises* and contemplated them with the senses of their whole being. Each saw with the eyes of his imagination, heard with the ears of his imagination, experienced intensely through smell, taste, and feeling the horrors of Hell and the raptures of Heaven, witnessed the battle between the armies of Christ and the armies of Satan, and followed every recorded detail of the life of Christ, from Bethlehem to Calvary.

Ignatius had left instructions to the director that the *Exercises* must be adapted to the age, capacity, and powers of those who undertook them, and that too heavy a burden should never be placed on a spirit still unenlightened or a heart still weak.

At the end of his retreat young Teilhard, now called Brother Pierre, and wearing the somber clerical garments, met his fellow novices. Close friendships were frowned upon during this period, for all had entered as equals and must be treated as such by classmates and teachers alike. But many a friendship developed later that had its beginning at the novitiate.

There was no time for picking up pebbles, as Teilhard called it, or even for thinking about them those first two years. More time was spent in fasting, prayer, and meditation than in study. Much of a Jesuit novice's training was influenced by the personal experiences of the Society's founder. The boys were put to work at menial tasks, as

Ignatius had done, to teach them the virtue of humility and obedience. When they made confession it was not only for their transgressions, but for all their secret instincts and impulses. They were sent out in pairs and penniless on pilgrimages to certain churches in France, depending on monasteries along the way for their food and lodging. Over and over they were reminded that a Jesuit priest must have constancy of character, virtue, prudence, and learning.

Ignatius had not planned to establish a religious order of the kind that existed in his day, groups of men isolated from the world behind monastery walls. After making a pilgrimage to Jerusalem he decided that, as a soldier of Christ, he must be a part of the world if he were to combat the evils in it. First he felt the need of a better education and, at the age of thirty-three, he began a period of study that lasted twelve years.

Wherever he went he attracted followers. In Paris he and six brilliant fellow students took vows of poverty and chastity and formed themselves into a group they called the Company of Jesus, later changing the name to the Society of Jesus. Within five years the following had grown so that, with the approval of the Pope, the members were organized into regional companies, or provinces, each with a Provincial at the head and local superiors under him. Ignatius was elected by the members as the General over all the provinces. The vow of obedience was then added to those of poverty and chastity. It was not meant as a servile obedience, but the kind a soldier shows to his commander, or a son to his father.

The novices training for priesthood in the Society were closely observed, and their traits of character, strong points as well as weak, were recorded. If one proved to be un-qualified, he could be dismissed. On the other hand, if one decided during this period that this was not his vocation after all, he could leave the order at any time he chose. Pierre, like his fellow novices, had entered only after careful consideration and prayer, and it was a choice he was never to regret.

When his training as a novice was finished, he was sent to Laval, near the northwest coast of France, for the second period of preparation. He took his first simple vows in March 1901. "I, Pierre, vow to Thy divine Majesty, *Poverty, Chastity,* and *Perpetual Obedience* to the Society of Jesus, and promise I will enter the same Society to live in it perpetually."

"At last I am a Jesuit," he wrote to his parents the same day. He hadn't time for more than a note, but he wanted them to know how happy he was in his choice. "If you only knew the joy I feel, now that I have given myself completely and forever to the Society, particularly at a time when she is being persecuted."

A long-standing feud between the French government and the Church had flared up again. After a heated debate in Parliament, an act had been passed calling for strict regulation of religious orders.

Discipline was more relaxed for the juniors than for the novices. Restrictions on close friendships were lifted, and Pierre became part of a group of bright young students with active, searching minds. Their studies in literature and languages were stimulating after the long months of emphasis on the *Spiritual Exercises.* Pierre, already a good classical scholar, composed poems in Latin and Greek and wrote a short play in Greek, in the style of Aristophanes' *Frogs,* which the students performed for their own amusement. But the atmosphere in the school was tense that year, with the uncertainty of what the government, under a new prime minister, would do next.

In the summer of 1901 an announcement was made that all religious orders would be abolished and education would be taken over by the State. For the third time in a twenty-five-year period, the Jesuits of France went into exile.

The students and staff at Laval were transferred to the island of Jersey in the English Channel. To avoid attracting attention, they decided against wearing clerical clothes. Their families hastily sent boxes of clothing, which they divided among themselves. Later they could look back with amusement at what a spectacle they had been in their hurried departure. Dignified fathers and serious young students were dressed in such odd assortments as a high silk hat and a light gray jacket, a long frock coat and a worn old derby hat, a formal morning coat and a motoring cap.

The Jesuits had two colleges in Jersey. At Bon Secours Pierre and his classmates continued their junior studies, and from there they went to the nearby Maison St. Louis for their scholastic work in science and philosophy.

Pierre was fascinated by the rocky headlands of Jersey, the cliffs rising sheer above the water's edge, the rock-strewn grottoes, the species of stone new to him. He wanted to know everything about the island's geology, and this brought on an inner struggle. He asked himself: Was this absorbing passion for nature in conflict with his religious dedication? Should he not give up all thought of the material and devote himself entirely to the spiritual? He went to one of the fathers for advice, and it was explained to him that to a Jesuit the claims of God and the world were not necessarily opposed, that pious behavior and innocent pleasure were by no means incompatible. "God looks as much for the natural development of your being as for its sanctification," the father said.

From then on, for the rest of his stay in Jersey, Pierre

Teilhard spent his holidays and as much time as he could spare between classes exploring the island.

"Brother Teilhard never goes for a walk without his hammer and magnifying glass," a classmate said.

He could look back on this as his time of preliminary investigations of the earth. He found he was not alone in his interests. Often he was accompanied by some of his fellow students, and the samples they collected and the observations they made were passed on to well-known geologists and paleontologists. During Pierre's last year there, Brother Félix Pelletier, a graduate in chemistry and mineralogy, collaborated with him on an article on the stones and minerals of the island for the local annual bulletin the Jesuits put out.

In 1905, when his scholastic studies were finished, Teilhard was ready for his next period of training. The official orders were issued around the middle of August, and Teilhard learned, to his surprise, that he would be sent to Egypt for three years, where he would teach chemistry and physics at the Jesuit secondary school in Cairo. His ship, *Congo,* would sail from Marseilles in eight days. This gave him time for a short visit with his family at Sarcenat.

It had been seven years since he left home to begin his studies for the priesthood. So much had happened during that time that the joy of the reunion was mingled with sorrow. There had been two deaths in the family. In the autumn of 1902, Albéric, then an officer in the French navy, had died at Sarcenat. Two years later, Louise had died of meningitis at the age of twelve. Guiguite had become permanently bedridden following an attack of pleurisy in the year of Albéric's death. The older sister, Françoise, was preparing to enter the order of the Little Sisters of the Poor, and would soon be leaving home.

The years had made a change in the five younger brothers. Pierre still called them by their childhood nicknames. Gabriel and Olivier were Biel and Yé Yé. They and Joseph were young men now and making plans for their careers. Gonzague would soon leave for the Jesuit school in Jersey. Only the youngest, Victor, called To To, was still being taught at home.

Pierre would always feel reluctant to leave Sarcenat. "But this is no longer where I should be, and it wouldn't be right to stay on," he said.

Each of the four Jesuit provinces of France was responsible for certain missions in other parts of the world. The province of Lyons had charge of those in the Middle East, in Armenia, Syria, and in Egypt at Alexandria and Cairo. There had been a reunion at Marseilles with friends he had known during his years of training. On the ship he shared a second-class cabin with three of them, and in Egypt he would find others.

Egypt fascinated Teilhard from the time the ship anchored at Alexandria. "I am dazzled by everything I have seen in the last few hours," he wrote at the end of a letter started on shipboard. "I am surprised anew each time I look out of a window and see above the square houses gilded with a magnificent light, great palm trees laden with green dates."

Frédéric de Bélinay, who had given up a military career to become a priest, had started as a novice with Teilhard at Aix. He was now teaching at the Jesuit school in Alexandria, and was getting together a natural history collection of shells, minerals, insects, and small animals. Since the schools were closed for the summer vacation, Teilhard remained for more than a week in Alexandria, spending part of his time helping de Bélinay organize his small museum. De Bélinay talked about his home in France, the large, rambling house and gardens, the mountains and forests and country lanes. To Teilhard there came memories of Sarcenat.

When he reached his final destination, the Holy Family College, a Jesuit secondary school in Cairo, Teilhard found other friends. Bovier-Lapierre, a fellow student who had gone on geological excursions with him in Jersey, arrived a few days later. Since the new school year would not start for another month, the two young naturalists had time to go exploring with hammer and sack.

The landscape, with its changing colors under a cloudless sky, was in complete contrast to the misty gray of the Channel Islands. The Nile, approaching the flood season, was red and opaque, bordered by a green screen of palms. The distant hills, yellow in the sunlight, faded to a deep purple in the evening glow.

"The East flowed over me in a first wave of exoticism. I gazed at it and drank it in eagerly—the country itself, not its peoples or its history (which as yet held no interest for me), but its light, its vegetation, its fauna, its deserts," he wrote, looking back on those first weeks in Egypt.

Everywhere there were reminders of an ancient past. He saw women drawing water in earthen jars from the canal and he thought of the biblical Rebecca at the well. The bleak, jagged hills in the region of the Red Sea were like illustrations in a book about the Holy Land his father had in his library at Sarcenat. At Giza the Pyramids and Sphinx loomed gigantic at the desert's edge, as in the time of the Pharaohs. But Pierre Teilhard's interest lay in a far older period of earth's history, millions of years before the Pharaohs.

He collected fossil oyster shells and sea urchins that covered the rock cliffs, and he found a rare kind of prehensile fish teeth, shaped like a cat's claw. He made notes of stones in the desert and hills: flint, sandstone, agate. Embedded in some of the stones were fossil prints of creatures that had lived in the remote past, long before the appearance of man.

Teilhard was also interested in the living things he saw about him. There were plants, birds, and insects familiar to him only through descriptions he had read. Others he did not recognize and could only guess at their identity. He had a chameleon sent to Sarcenat so the family could observe its changes in color, and he found an agama, something between a lizard and a chameleon, which he took to his room to raise. The butterflies he saw hovering around the flowers in a garden were like the rare Vanessa butterfly in the collection at Sarcenat. And a black click beetle he discovered was as large as the red one at home.

The students began arriving during the last week in September, and on the following Wednesday Teilhard held his first class in chemistry and physics. He walked into the room to face the dark eyes of thirty-five students gazing seriously at him. He wondered if he would ever learn their names, which were pronounced in sounds so unfamiliar to his ears. And how could he present his ideas in a way that their young minds would understand?

The days passed quickly, for he discovered that there was nothing like teaching to give one a thirst for study. He had the class start raising silkworms. They studied the caterpillar and larvae found on the leaves of a desert mimosa, and they went on field trips, searching for stones and fossils. The bored expressions that first greeted Teilhard gradually changed to interest and enthusiasm. One student in the class was later to become a well-known entomologist and secretary of the Egyptian Entomological Society.

Pierre Teilhard had a class for older boys in humanities, rhetoric, and philosophy. In addition, by having charge of the altar boys, and supervising the bus trips to pick up the day students and take them home in the evening, he had a chance to become acquainted with students other than those in his classes.

There were fifteen day students, all around To To's age, and in many ways they reminded him of his ten-year-old brother. Beneath his dignified clerical garments and his newly acquired beard, he secretly shared the boys' excitement in the bus ride through the streets of Cairo. They saw some Arabs leading dog-faced baboons on a leash. Caravans of camels came ambling by from time to time, swaying from side to side under great loads of sugar cane.

One morning the Khedive, the Turkish viceroy of Egypt, came riding by in a large yellow automobile. With his turbaned head held high, he had the air of one accustomed to rule. He was escorted by a guard mounted on magnificent gray horses and carrying lances with green streamers. They, like the Khedive, wore turbans of silk wrapped around a red felt fez. The bus driver, trying to take advantage of an opening, was caught in the rear of the convoy. Teilhard found himself, in the rattletrap of a bus, riding between two rows of respectful Arabs and a cordon of police. His regret was that none of the students had been picked up yet. This would have given them something to talk about for weeks.

The school had a natural history museum of sorts, and Teilhard lost no time in putting it in order. His Sundays and holidays were spent searching for interesting specimens to add to it. He and Lapierre went on their first camel ride to a fossil bed in the Libyan desert, some distance beyond the Pyramids, where the sand made walk-

ing almost impossible. They had expected a feeling of
seasickness from the animal's swaying motion, but they
found the slow and easy rhythm restful instead. The
camel's expression, with its pendulous lips and big, shining
eyes, amused them. It grumbled and snorted with every
extra effort, and had to be appeased with crusts of bread
and cheese, orange peels, and whatever green vegetation
they could find.

Donkeys were also used on some of the excursions into
the hilly regions. They presented a different kind of problem. The two Jesuits were never sure whether they would
be pitched over the heads of their mounts, or when the
donkeys would come to a halt and refuse stubbornly to
move.

Lapierre was in Egypt for no more than a year, but
Teilhard did not lack companions on his excursions. In
writing to a friend about his latest finds he said: "These
results show what one can do between classroom duties and
the various school chores, if one takes the trouble to find a
companion who doesn't mind spending the only free day
in the week turning over stones right out in the desert, or
detaching some big fossil from a rocky wall, in heat like a
furnace."

The Egyptians were constantly amazed to see this tall,
dignified Jesuit, obviously aristocratic, picking up grass-
hoppers, lizards, and caterpillars to put in containers,
hammering with infinite care at a rock, or standing bare-
foot in the black silt of the Nile prying sea-urchin fossils
from the limestone. Heads turned when he walked
through the streets of Cairo on a very hot day, cradling in
his hands a rock as big as a man's head. An especially fine
vertebra of a long-extinct marine mammal was embedded
so firmly in the rock that he was taking it back to his room
to extract at leisure.

Sometimes he was suspected of digging for ancient treasures to be sent out of the country, and officials demanded to see his papers. Once a poor peasant came close and looked on in curiosity while he gently hammered at a rock. When he saw only a tiny fossil being extracted as if it were a precious gem, he began shaking with laughter. And Pierre Teilhard joined him.

He had the enthusiasm of a boy in his delight over each new discovery. When he was in doubt about identification, he was helped by naturalist friends he had made in Cairo. Dr. Innes, director of the medical school at Cairo University, had a very fine natural history collection, with every kind of shell, beetle, butterfly, or bird he could find in Egypt. Another friend, René Fourtau, was an engineer from France, and also a geologist. Eventually, Teilhard was able to contribute findings of his own to his friends' collections. In the desert of the Suez he discovered a very odd species of grasshopper. This would add to the future work of Innes, he said. And from upper Egypt he brought back sea urchins of a kind that delighted Fourtau, who was writing an article about them.

Though he considered himself still an amateur, Pierre Teilhard's reputation as a scientist grew during his three years in Egypt. Occasionally visitors connected with the French Geological Society or the Natural History Museum of Paris came to Cairo. Under Teilhard's guidance they were able to take back celestite crystals, shells, cocoons, and fossils—all rare and some even unknown to them. In lectures and in articles of scientific publications there was mention of Teilhard and the work he was doing in the natural history of Egypt. The fossil fishes' teeth he sent to Paris included a new species and three new varieties. One was called Teilhardi in his honor. Fourtau, in his article on sea urchins of Egypt, wrote of Teilhard's work in discovering two new species and eight new varieties. Fourtau gave the name Teilhardi to one of these.

In early July 1908, there were final examinations at the Holy Family School, followed by the ceremony of prize-giving. Then Teilhard had to wait until the middle of August to find out about his next move. During the few weeks he had left in Egypt he crowded in as many trips as he could to favorite places in hills, deserts, and along the lakesides. "Not without melancholy," he wrote to his parents, "because I am less sure than Father that my fate next year will not be to pace the cliffs of Hastings."

The last week in July was spent in retreat, then the young Jesuits went to Alexandria to wait for their orders. Teilhard took a train to the desert adjoining Lake Mairiut, another of his favorite spots. Egypt would be hard to leave. It was here he had discovered in the rock fossils of low forms of life, creatures long extinct. Also, during an unforgettable journey of eight days in the Faiyum region of Egypt, he had seen the bones of strange, enormous animals of a far distant past. All these turned his thoughts to the world's slow state of change.

His prediction about his fate for the coming year had been right. When the orders arrived he accepted obediently, as he would always do. By the middle of September he was at Ore Place, a Jesuit house in Hastings, on the Sussex coast of England, to begin his four years' study of theology. "But Egypt is hard to forget," he wrote soon after his arrival.

He had stopped off at Sarcenat on his way for a brief visit with his family, and he made another stop at Amiens, where Françoise was working with the Little Sisters of the Poor in a home for the aged.

"I hope life in Cairo hasn't tired him out too much," Françoise wrote to her parents, telling of his visit. "He has lost weight, but is happy nonetheless. You should be very proud of him. He is kinder than ever before, and is still as good and serious as ever."

Pierre was as concerned about her. Guiguite had said that Françoise was nailed down by too much austerity. But after seeing Françoise he did not agree. It was at the end of a retreat for the old people, and his sister received him in the kitchen, where they ate and visited, telling each other of the things that had happened during their three years' separation. Françoise seemed happy in her vocation. Pierre met some of the old men under her care, and he stayed to chant the office with the community. But when he left he had the uneasy feeling that something was hanging over her head.

In Hastings, as in Jersey and Egypt, old friends were united. Frédéric de Bélinay was there, and two others Pierre was especially pleased to see, August Valensin and Pierre Charles.

His theological studies kept him more confined than he had been since leaving the novitiate. There were discussions with Valensin and Charles. Their modern approach, more in keeping with the present century than the medieval theology of the textbooks, helped clear up questions that were beginning to form in his mind.

"Theology makes me think about a lot of things," Teilhard wrote to his parents. "I am beginning to see that there are so many other questions, less appealing, perhaps, but more vital than the sciences, that I am beginning to wonder if I shall be sidetracked one day or another."

He had classes in fundamental theology and in moral theology. There were preparations for the theological disputes held at the end of every school year. These were given in Latin and conducted in the same way they had been for centuries. The first year Teilhard had to challenge his professor's theses, and the next three years he had to defend them. This meant knowing and absorbing the subject well.

At the same time Teilhard was beginning to see the universe in its oneness. The subject of evolution was being bitterly argued in the pulpits and lecture halls, and misunderstood as often on one side as the other. The word came to Teilhard's mind like a refrain, a promise, a summons, something desired. Looking at the solid English countryside, at sunset especially, the Sussex woods seemed charged with all the fossil life he had been looking for. "Sometimes it really seemed to me as though suddenly some sort of universal being was about to take on shape in nature before my very eyes," he wrote forty years later.

He wrote little of his studies to his parents, or of the ideas taking shape in his mind. Instead he gave detailed descriptions of the things that impressed him, an albino pheasant, a formation of storks flying, the gilded tops of birches and beeches in autumn, the fossils discovered in his walks with de Bélinay and Félix Pelletier during a rare period of leisure. His letters showed an intense love of the earth, and often an expression of happiness in his chosen vocation.

Teilhard and his naturalist companions made the most of the little spare time they had by exploring the woods and the cliffs and quarries in the immediate neighborhood. In this chalky soil, formed about 120 million years before, there were bones of giant reptiles and early mammals. A few days after his arrival at Hastings, Teilhard found leaf impressions embedded in the rocks along the cliffs. And in the crumbling rocks along the Sussex coast he discovered a dozen or so footprints of the iguanodon. This gigantic species of dinosaur, sometimes as tall as thirty feet, had walked on two bird-like feet. The prints Teilhard found were of three large digits between eight and eleven inches long.

About once a month the young Jesuits were allowed to take an all-day excursion over the countryside. De Bélinay knew the region so well that on one of these trips he and Teilhard walked forty kilometers. But it was not until nine months after his studies at Hastings began that he was able to explore the chalky cliffs he could see on the horizon from the window of his room. It was during the vacation for Pentecost, and he spent the whole day there. His collection of fossil plants grew until eventually it became an important contribution to the British Museum. An article about the plants was published in the journal of the Geological Society of London. Two plants, previously unknown, were given his name.

Teilhard's interest, however, was more in the fauna than the flora of England. In Jersey he had made a study of the geological structure of the island and his collection was of stones. In Egypt his search had been for fossil shells and insects. Now he turned to later forms of life, the dinosaurs, the mammals that replaced them, and from these to early man.

On one excursion he met Charles Dawson, an attorney and amateur geologist. Dawson was supervising some digging at an old quarry, where Teilhard thought he was the manager until the talk turned to fossils. Dawson had just discovered the enormous pelvic bone of an iguanodon. He showed Teilhard and his companion his other discoveries, fragments of bones found piece by piece until he had almost enough to reconstruct a complete iguanodon. They were being carefully packed in a crate for the British Museum. After that Teilhard began supplying Dawson with fossils wanted by the museum, including teeth from a small crocodile that had not yet been found in that region.

In August of his third year at Ore Place, twelve years after he had started his training, Pierre Teilhard was ordained a priest. From now on he would be known as Father Teilhard and no longer as Brother Pierre. His parents and four of his brothers were there for the ceremony. Olivier, a mining engineer, was on an expedition in Mexico, and Guiguite's confinement kept her from joining them. The day after the ordination, Father Teilhard said his first Mass. The Mass was served by Gabriel and Joseph. His father and brothers wore black bands on their sleeves, and his mother was dressed in black with the mourning veil she was so often to wear. News had come only two months before that Françoise, who had been sent to work with the Little Sisters of the Poor in Shanghai, had died suddenly of smallpox.

"It seemed an interminably long time before ordination day arrived. So pass all things, the best as the saddest," Teilhard wrote after his parents and brothers returned to Sarcenat. He had wanted to express the great affection he felt when he was with them. "Just the same, you know what I meant," he added.

As a priest he now had spiritual duties in addition to his studies. He was sent to nearby parishes or convents to celebrate Mass, to preach and hear confessions. The day finally arrived when he attended his last class, March 22, 1912. Afterwards he was given a list of various questions on theology and philosophy, and he spent the next four months in independent study, working out the answers on his own from all that he had been taught over the years. Though this meant intensive concentration and work, the older students had talked about how pleasant it was to be in a house where classes were held and not have to attend.

Father Teilhard was in the midst of his studies when,

in April, Charles Dawson came to visit him. He brought with him some prehistoric fossils that workmen had found near Piltdown in a bed of gravel deposited by some long-forgotten river. There were bones of elephant and hippopotamus and a thick, well-preserved fragment of a human skull, chocolate-brown in color. With these he tried to tempt Teilhard into joining him on an expedition. It was impossible for Teilhard to get away then, but a month later, when he was sent to the village of Bramber for two weeks of priestly duties, he stopped on his way to visit Dawson at his home. The house was built inside the ruins of an old castle overlooking the town of Lewes.

After a hearty English breakfast with Dawson and his wife, the two men set off for the village of Uckfield, where they were joined by Sir Arthur Smith-Woodward, curator of the geology department of the British Museum. From there they drove to the gravel bed, where they worked with picks and sifters for several hours. Dawson discovered a new fragment of the pieces of human skull he had already found. Teilhard picked up a piece of an elephant's molar. Woodward, a small, graying man who until then had seemed rather cold, reached for it enthusiastically. "I had the same feeling a hunter has over his first goose," Teilhard said. He had to leave to meet his train, but the other men were still hard at work in their search.

In July, as the final examination and the last thesis to be disputed drew near, the young priests at Ore Place started packing their few belongings to leave, with no sure knowledge but only hints and speculations of where they would go.

Woodward came down from London to visit Father Teilhard and to look over his collection of animal and plant fossils. "He has plundered my collection enough to make me feel flattered," Teilhard wrote. He later received an acknowledgment of receipt from the British Museum, handsomely engraved on parchment.

Just before his examination on July 14th, Teilhard was given a schedule of what he would do the following month, while waiting for a definite assignment to come through. He would leave on the 16th for Paris to stay for four days. While there he would call on Marcellin Boule, professor of paleontology at the Museum of Natural History. From this he knew that his future would be in science. "The East doesn't seem to be on my list for the coming year," he said with some regret. From Paris he would go to Lyons to conduct a retreat for students, then make his own retreat. After August 5th he would be free to go to Sarcenat and wait for the official order.

III
Paris

As a Jesuit, Pierre Teilhard's period of training was still not over after he had earned the equivalent of a doctor's degree in theology through four years of study. His first, simple vows were taken at the end of two years as a novice. Now he had to spend one more year in prayer and meditation, as a tertian, before taking the solemn, final vows.

The superiors of the Order wisely take into account the talents and personality of each individual and, with an eye to his future, they make the decisions for the year's assignments. Throughout the Society's long history, Jesuits have been chosen to serve in the way they are considered most capable. They have been teachers, writers, scientists. Some have acted as confessors and advisers to heads of state. Others have gone out to establish missions in all parts of the world, however remote and isolated. Some have gone east as far as Japan. Others accompanied the early explorers to the New World, sharing the dangers and hardships of an unknown land and people.

Pierre Teilhard's intense interest in geology and prehistory had not gone unnoticed. It was decided to postpone his tertianship for a year so that he could work toward a doctorate in science. When the orders were received on August 15th, that memorable day of the year for a Jesuit in training, Teilhard was not surprised to learn that he would study under Marcellin Boule in his laboratory at the Museum of Natural History in Paris. He had felt the call of the East, but it was also good to live in his own country again. Except for a few brief visits, he had spent the past eleven years in exile, but now the attitude of the government toward the Jesuits had become a little more tolerant.

During his first weeks in Paris it seemed to Father Teilhard that he was spending most of his time going from one place to another. He had a room on the fifth floor of one Jesuit house and took his meals at another a few blocks away. He began his day by saying Mass at six o'clock at the Abbaye-aux-Bois and ended it, after a late evening meal, with his third long climb up the five flights of stairs to his room. The recently built Paris subway had a station practically at the door of the Jesuit house. From his window Teilhard could hear, above the noise and bustle of the busy street corner, the roar of an underground train every five minutes. But off in the distance there rose the towers of St. Sulpice.

His brother Victor was attending school in Paris, and the two of them often had dinner together at a favorite restaurant of the students. The other brothers came through from time to time. Pierre called on his Uncle Georges, whom he hadn't seen in eighteen years. He found him sitting contentedly before the fire eating bonbons. He met his uncle's wife and young son and daughter for the first time. "It was a real Teilhard place," he wrote his family. "The children even spoke the same way I did as a child."

His Aunt Pauline and her daughter were living in a suburb of Paris. When he visited her she reminded him of the practical jokes he had played as a child. She still remembered the frog he had put in her bedroom at her country home Vernière, though he had long forgotten it. But the place he called "that little corner of Clermont" was the home of Uncle Cirice and Aunt Marie, who had moved with their family to Paris a few years earlier.

On his first visit he had been a little saddened to see how his uncle had aged. He would never have recognized the younger children, Alice and Robert, and he knew Marcel, then an electrical engineer, only because of a photograph Gabriel had shown him. Marguerite and Jeanne, the two oldest, brought back memories of their childhood together at Fontfreyde. Marguerite, a woman of exceptional intelligence and charm, was thirty-two, five months older than Pierre. For the past eight years she had been in charge of a Catholic boarding school for girls. When the state secondary schools for girls were established, she had realized that if the private schools were to continue, they would have to raise the standard of education and teach more than the basic subjects and how to embroider and play the piano. Also, better qualified teachers would be needed. To prepare for this she had worked for a degree at the Sorbonne, which was unusual for a woman at that time.

She and Pierre were drawn together, at this first reunion as adults, by more than the ties of kinship. A friendship, both spiritual and intellectual, developed that would last throughout their lives. "It was like the friendship between brother and sister," Marguerite described it.

She had admired her two cousins, Françoise and Marguerite-Marie, one for her devotion and sacrifice as a Little Sister of the Poor, the other for her spiritual serenity in suffering. She, too, wanted to live a life of piety, but she could not feel the call to join a religious order. Time and again, in the years to follow, Pierre would comfort her with the assurance that she would find spiritual development in the work she was doing.

Marcellin Boule returned from his vacation to find Pierre Teilhard busy becoming acquainted with the museum, working and studying in the library of the paleontological laboratory. Boule, a native of Auvergne, was entirely different from his new student. He was short and heavy-set, with a reputation of being quick-tempered, sarcastic, and dictatorial. But he was brilliant in his field of paleontology. He was one of the few specialists on Neanderthal man, and was the first to reconstruct a complete Neanderthal skeleton.

The museum had acquired a collection of early mammal fossils from Quercy in the southwest of France. Boule turned these over to Teilhard to make a study of their origins for his project. Learning to identify fragments of bones and teeth and to fit them together was slow and tedious at first. "I've almost grasped the physiognomy of the jawbone," Teilhard wrote a month after beginning his studies. He had seen fossils of huge mammals at Faiyum in Egypt, but there had been no time to examine them. Now he was able to study more closely the Eocene period, going back to the time, over 50 million years ago, when mammals were making their first appearance in a reptilian world. This resulted in two of his important published papers, one on the Carnivora and the other on the Primates of the phosphorites of Quercy. The Eocene period would also form the basis of his doctoral dissertation.

Bones were coming into the museum from faraway Siberia as well as the nearby zoo, the Jardin des Plantes. When an animal died there it was sent to the laboratory for dissection and study. The shelves of the laboratory were filled with bottles of bones preserved in alcohol, permeating the place with a sickly odor. Teilhard compared the smell to that of a dead rat in a sewer. "Just wait until the corpse of a hippopotamus comes in," a more experienced laboratory assistant said.

In November Teilhard began classes at the Catholic Institute and the College of France, in addition to his work at the museum. He found them more or less a repetition of things he already knew. The lectures at the Geological Institute, which he had joined, and discussions with friends he had made among the members were much more stimulating.

In addition to his studies, Teilhard was assigned the usual spiritual duties of a priest. Every other week he went by streetcar and subway to Borget, outside Paris, where he said Mass for a group of homeless waifs. The owner of a glass factory had established an orphanage to take them in from the streets and had given them work so they could learn a trade. When Teilhard made a tour of the ovens and saw the boys at work forming various shapes and sizes of crystal decanters, he sensed a loneliness about them that he had never known. During Lent and on summer holidays he was sent to small parishes. At first he worried over his sermons, working painstakingly until he was satisfied. "But that still does not give me the inclination to become a preacher," he said.

Father Teilhard, with his quiet dignity, gracious and obliging, yet as unyielding as stone in what he believed was right, was able to win over the quick-tempered Boule. Boule recognized in him the qualities a first-rate naturalist should have—the ability to work hard, a keen sense of observation and analysis, and, most important, a great independence of mind. "His career, though just begun, already gives promise of being among the most brilliant," he added.

Through Boule, Teilhard met other scientists interested in prehistory. Two were priests—Henri Breuil, a native of Normandy, and Hugo Obermaier, an Austrian—who could reconcile, as Father Teilhard was beginning to, the long and still continuing story of creation with their religion. Like Boule, Breuil had the short, sturdy build of a peasant. Both men were pioneers in the study of early man, each an expert in his chosen field. But in temperament they were entirely different. Breuil was vivacious and cheerful, easy to know. A warm friendship sprang up between him and Teilhard at their first meeting. "He showed me some wonderful things (stone tools, carved and sketched-out bones) which he had just found in Spain, and has shown himself to be most friendly. Perhaps I will learn the most from him," Teilhard wrote to his parents after the meeting.

As a seminary student, Breuil had been encouraged by one of his professors to take up a scientific career. His first interest had been in the Bronze Age, but from there he went to a much earlier period of man's development, when he lived in caves and his only tools were fashioned out of the stones and bones he found about him. Breuil made a study of these caves, then being rediscovered in France and Spain. He was especially interested in the paintings and carvings on walls and ceilings, and he made detailed copies of them. By 1912, when Teilhard met him, he had already published three books, with his own illustrations, on the caves he had examined.

A book by Obermaier, entitled *Prehistoric Man,* had also been published recently. It was the first volume in a series, "Man in All Ages," on the most recent discoveries of anthropology, to be written by Catholic scholars and published in Germany.

Little by little Teilhard's own belief had been growing in his mind. It began at Hastings with his first awareness of the fossilized life that filled the Sussex forests and the sense of a universal being taking shape there. "I was far from understanding it and clearly evaluating the importance of the change that was taking place in me," he said. It had come less as an abstract notion than as a presence that was gradually enveloping his whole being. Now with his studies under Boule, and the exchange of ideas with new friends he was making, the path before him became clear.

An essay he wrote on Obermaier's book was published in January 1913 by the Jesuit magazine *Etudes.* "Now that a calmer view of the relations between science and faith shows that religious truth is safe from any turns that the experimental science of Man may take, it would be unpardonable to ignore or inveigh against the work of the prehistorians," Teilhard said. Obermaier took his reader down the still unfamiliar roads of prehistory, telling where the oldest traces of man could be found, how they could be dated, and what they revealed of the life of early man. He pictured the period of tropical warmth before the last glacial age, when nomads roamed the plains of western Europe hunting the elephant and bison, and the rivers were bordered with fig trees and laurels. Then, with the advance of the ice, the tropical animals departed for warmer regions, and the lemmings, reindeer, and mammoths began coming down from the north. Man had to go to the caves for shelter against the cold; he covered himself with animal skins and learned to make fire for warmth. He left no trace of his existence in the open air, but the caves, preserving his remains, his tools, and the ashes of his fires, tell the story of his progress.

Father Teilhard was invited to take part in an expedition in June 1913 to explore the caves in northwest Spain. In the group were Obermaier; his young Alsatian assistant; an Englishman, the son of a Cambridge professor; and an American, an expert on Pre-Columbian civilization. Breuil promised to join them at the end of the month.

They were full of energy and enthusiasm and thought nothing of climbing the high hills where the caves were located, then working with pickax and bare hands from early morning until late evening. Teilhard was dressed as the others, in shirtsleeves and open collar and wearing the sandals of the region. Only by his clerical hat, pushed back on his head, could he have been recognized as a priest.

Ancient man chose for his home caves well hidden from view, on hills so steep they were almost impossible to climb. His living quarters were at the entrance, or hall of the cave only. Different stages of man's development can be traced by digging through layers of carbon separated one from another by thick chalk deposits.

At the first cave explored by the young scientists, eight of the twelve layers had been uncovered. There they painstakingly lifted out bone splinters and whole bones and teeth. They were able to identify bones of deer, rhinoceros, horse, ibex, bear, lion, and hyena. To their disappointment they found no remains of ancient man, although he had left his tools of carved animal bones.

The back of the cave's entrance opened into a long grotto. There, in the farthest corner, could be seen the cave dwellers' drawings and paintings. These also showed the different periods of man's progress. Some were as clumsily drawn as a child's first efforts. Others showed an understanding of an animal's anatomy and a sense of movement. One wall was mysteriously covered with pictures of hands. The left hand had obviously been held against the wall while a finger of the right hand, dipped in red ocher, traced around it, then filled in the spaces between the fingers so that the hand stood out white against a red background.

Father Teilhard went back into the grotto for another look, alone and in a silence broken only by the sound of drops falling from stalactites. There was much here to meditate upon in the presence of traces of a mankind earlier than any known civilization.

In this rocky part of Spain are several places where early man had found shelter. Obermaier jokingly spoke of one as an inn, and gave it the name Zur Krote, meaning "At the Sign of the Frog." The group was photographed having lunch at the entrance. Other photographs showed them at work, or sitting down to rest, still holding their pickaxes, looking tired but contented.

The most famous of the caves was at Altamira, a coal-mining town by the sea. Bear tracks could be seen on the stalagmites and even in the soft clay, and on the ceiling there were magnificent pictures of bison painted in red, yellow, and black. Each was about seven feet long and well preserved. In three of them the artist had taken advantage of the natural curves in the rock and had drawn the animals in bold positions. One, especially haunting, was pictured in the act of charging, its eyes livid with rage.

A mining engineer had discovered the cave in 1875, and had been impressed by the bone and flint tools he found there. On a later visit his small daughter, who had accompanied him, was the first to notice the pictures of animals overhead. The scientists of the time refused to believe in the antiquity of the discoveries. The paintings were recent forgeries, they said, or perhaps the work of Roman soldiers stationed there in Caesar's time. Then, one after another, caves with wall drawings and carvings were discovered in France and Spain, and a new generation was now prepared to accept the fact of their great age.

The Abbé Breuil had visited the cave at Altamira in 1902 and made copies of the pictures, which were the subject of one of his books. He was the first to point out that here, as in the other known caves, the works of art had been made in the remotest, most hard-to-reach parts of the caverns. Hidden behind rocks or in narrow niches, they could not have been intended as mere decorations. They obviously held a religious significance, evidence of man's early groping toward God, a way of prayer to a higher power looked up to in both fear and reverence. Was this a sort of holy of holies? Father Teilhard wondered as he looked up at them. What did these paintings mean to their primitive creators? "This is quite disturbing," he wrote to his parents a few days later. "I must confess I did not go back there again."

On his way back to Paris he stopped off at Lourdes, where Guiguite had come so often with her mother, fervently hoping for a cure. He said Mass in the Basilica, but he found it difficult to pray quietly in the grotto because of the crowds. In the office of verification a doctor showed him a few cases of improvements on file, although, with perhaps one exception, no definite cures. But the sight of the pilgrims kneeling in earnest prayer, the devotion of the stretcher-bearers, and the Procession of the Blessed Sacrament moved him deeply.

In Paris Teilhard found himself in a whirlpool of activity, catching up with his research work. He made drawings and photographs of bones and rocks and organized the notes for his thesis. At the end of the academic year, the last week in July, he learned that he would spend August and September in England. He would go first to Canterbury, then to Ore Place, where he would make his retreat from August 15th to 24th. From there he would go to Jersey to spend the rest of his vacation. It would seem strange to return to these familiar places, not as a student, but as a priest and a theologian.

At the end of his stay at Canterbury, Teilhard stopped off at Lewes to visit Charles Dawson at his ivy-covered villa, where he was treated as one of the family. The Dawsons' son, home on leave from Sudan, brought out pictures he had taken of the country. Mrs. Dawson proudly showed Teilhard her flower garden within the walls of the old castle, and he helped her cut sweet peas to arrange in vases. But the most exciting part of the visit was a return to the gravel beds of Piltdown. Dr. Woodward came down from London to join them, as he had when Teilhard was there last. The three men spent Friday afternoon, all day Saturday, and Sunday afternoon digging for fossils, but they found nothing except one small fragment of what might have been a nose.

The year before Dawson had found more portions of the human cranium and the lower part of an ape-like jaw that seemed to belong to it. This discovery caused a sensation among the world's scientists. If man was the result of evolution, there must have been a missing link between him and the animal, a creature with a human cranium and brain capacity and the body of an ape. And here it was. *Eoanthropus dawsoni,* or Dawson's dawn man, it was named, but it came to be known as the Piltdown man.

An exhibition of the Piltdown discoveries was being held in London by the Congress of Medical Anatomists. Teilhard was able to attend only the first session of discussions before going off for his retreat. At the second session, he was told, there had been criticism about the way Woodward had put the skull together. Teilhard agreed with those who wanted it reassembled in a new way. "But," he said, "in my opinion all these reconstructions aren't of much interest and don't add any certainty about it; other pieces have to be found."

Teilhard was the one who found the next piece. After his retreat was over, he was back at Piltdown digging with Dawson and Woodward. Embedded in the earth dug up by former excavations and washed by the rains was an eye tooth, ape-like in shape, but with the patterns of wear found only in human teeth. It was an exciting discovery, and proof to Woodward that his reconstruction had been right.

Marcellin Boule was one of the few scientists who refused to accept the authenticity of the Piltdown man. If the jaw was ape-like, he said, it was because it was an ape's jaw. The upper and lower parts of the skull were from two different creatures. Teilhard agreed that, living, it must have been a monstrosity, but he had no reason to doubt the integrity of his English friends. He was still at the learning stage of paleontology. The study itself was comparatively new, though by now the museums and libraries were being filled with prehistoric collections and publications on prehistory, and institutions had been founded for research on the subject.

Pierre Teilhard was back in Paris in October to begin his last year of study under Boule. After that, it had been decided, he would serve his tertianship in preparation for his final vows. It would be a year, like the two of his novitiate, devoted to asceticism, prayer, meditation, and contemplation of the *Spiritual Exercises;* following an initial thirty-day retreat.

His doctoral thesis on the phosphorites of Quercy needed only a few finishing touches. Teilhard spent a great deal of his time visiting archaeological museums, caves, and excavation sites throughout France studying Eocene fossils and strata. His thoughts went back to man's beginning and his long struggle forward. The Creator had implanted a lesson in the struggle, he wrote, a lesson in hard work and sturdy development.

On June 28, 1914, the news went out over the world that Francis Ferdinand, heir to the Austrian throne, had been assassinated with his wife by a Serb terrorist in protest against the seizure of his country. The people, reading their daily papers, little dreamed of how this event would affect their own lives. They went on with their daily affairs, unaware of the secret treaties and alliances their governments had formed, or of the expansion of munition plants and shipbuilding by the leading powers.

Pierre Teilhard wrote to his parents on that day, telling of his plans for a trip to the Alps with one of his teachers from the Catholic Institute to make a map of the Val d'Isere. At the beginning of summer vacation in July they were on their way, making their headquarters at the Jesuit house in Grenoble. For a week they hiked about the Alpine region of southeastern France close to the Italian border, wearing heavy overcoats and spiked shoes and carrying knapsacks on their backs. One day they climbed almost 10,000 feet, from four in the morning until eight at night, without feeling the least bit tired. They had never seen a more peaceful landscape, with clear, sparkling lakes, rhododendrons in bloom like a colorful rug beneath the larch trees, and from the valley below there came the sound of cowbells, in different tones that produced a serene and beautiful harmony. A light snow fell, settling on the ferns and outlining the tracks of woodchucks and mountain goats.

The next day came a downpour that lasted a week. Wheat fields were flooded up to the top of the plants, and mud slides isolated many of the towns around. Trains could not move and stations were crowded with stranded travelers and students on their way home for the holidays. Through the gray rain one could see an almost uninterrupted stream of French soldiers making for the Alpine forts on the Italian border.

On July 28th, after negotiations had failed, Austria declared war on Serbia. Russia began mobilizing troops to fight on Serbia's side. Germany, who had a secret pact with Austria, declared war on Russia August 1st. That same day the French Council of Ministers announced a general mobilization. Teilhard, who had not brought his military pass with him, managed to take the last train out of Grenoble before the order went into effect. Unlike his brothers and most of the young men of France, he had no regiment to report to. At twenty-one he had registered for noncombat duty and two years later he again registered, but he had not been called to military service. Now all he could do was stay in Paris and wait for his call, which he expected any day.

Germany declared war on France two days after the mobilization and sent her troops into neutral Belgium. The next day, August 4th, Britain declared war on Germany. Within one week half the countries of Europe were at war. Neither side thought the war would last more than a few months at the most, but it was to drag on for four and a half years, spreading over the entire world, at a cost of over 8 million lives.

After the fall of Belgium refugees began crossing the border and making their way to Paris. Later the wounded were brought in, and the sounds of gunfire came closer.

Weeks passed and still Father Teilhard received no call for military duty. He tried to enlist in the ambulance corps, but without success. His work with Boule in the almost deserted museum helped him through the suspense of waiting. Together they carefully packed the most valuable of the fossil treasures and put them away for safety. There was also work Teilhard could do with Marguerite and her assistant, Mme. Parion, who had turned their school into a shelter for the refugees.

Gloom settled over Paris. Each new edition of the newspapers, which kept coming out one right after the other, was read eagerly for the latest reports. Military cars filled the city streets and the explosion of bombs could be heard all during the night. "Please heaven that during these beautiful days, when they have time to think things over, the government will take steps to stop this dreadful plague that is upon us," Pierre Teilhard wrote to his parents on a day in late August.

He saw many of his fellow Jesuits leave to become chaplains in the army, and he longed to be among them, for anything was better than having to sit around and wait. All his brothers were in military service, even Victor, who was underage and had to volunteer. Olivier returned from Mexico to join his regiment. When he came through Paris the two brothers had a brief reunion after a separation of several years. Pierre Teilhard saw him off at the railway station, then returned to his room at the Jesuit house. There he found a note from his religious superiors. He was to follow the schedule planned before he started on his trip to the Alps and begin his tertian year at Canterbury on September 25th.

At the end of his thirty-day retreat, Teilhard received word that his brother Gonzague had been killed in action. Gonzague, who had so enjoyed his youth that he was reluctant to leave it and prepare for a future career as his brothers had done, was dead at the age of twenty.

"May God's will be done and may His kingdom be our final goal. This is the important thing," Pierre Teilhard wrote to his parents. In December he finally received his own call to service. He was assigned to the thirteenth division of the medical corps stationed at Clermont. A month later he was sent to the front as a stretcher-bearer, second-class, in a regiment of Moroccan and Algerian light infantry.

IV
A World at War

THE MEDICAL OFFICER of the regiment wrote of Teilhard's arrival at the front: "One morning . . . coming from Clermont-Ferrand, I saw, arriving by himself to serve as regimental stretcher-bearer, a young man whose clear eyes reflected intelligence and kindliness. In order to become more 'Arab' he had exchanged his field-service blue for the khaki of the African troops and his Kepi for a red fez. . . . Such was my first meeting with Father Teilhard."

War had not yet lost its glory in 1914. The heroes of history still were wartime leaders: the generals, prime ministers, and presidents. Little boys played with toy soldiers or fought mock battles. As young men, whatever their nationality, youth accepted without question the call to war, to a life of killing and being killed for what they were told was a just cause. France called for recruits from her many colonies and they obeyed. Those from Algeria and Morocco wore colorful Oriental uniforms, with baggy trousers tucked inside their boots. They had been drilled to perfection by their French officers.

Nothing in Pierre Teilhard's thirty-three years had prepared him for the life he was facing. He was strong, energetic, and had great physical and spiritual endurance, but he had gone from the security of a large, affectionate family to the sheltered life of a Jesuit scholar. His associations had been almost entirely with relatives, fellow priests, and scientists. Now, for the first time, he found himself on an equal footing with men of all kinds of background and intelligence. This enabled him to see himself as he never had before. "For us soldier-priests, war was a baptism into reality," he said. He felt part of the mass of mankind, united, yet with each individual a separate entity.

He lived the life of the enlisted man, sometimes in muddy dugouts, with the whistle of shells and the crack of bullets in his ears, and sometimes billeted in a barn on a Flemish field or the cellar of a bombed-out farmhouse, where the once prosperous land was pitted with shell holes and thick with the graves of those fallen in previous battles. He saw the best and the worst of man's behavior, supreme heroism and bestiality. He witnessed after each battle the pain of the wounded, followed by death or recovery, or mutilation that was neither life nor death.

The medical officer had Teilhard promoted to corporal after a few months of action. "Two features of his personality struck me immediately, his courage and his humility," he said. "He was the one I sent to the critical points of the battlefield, unless he went willingly of his own accord, for both the head of the medical corps, who appreciated his worth, and I had given him complete freedom to do his work best."

Father Teilhard was offered a more central station back at the billets but he decided this was not his place. He felt it was best to remain where he could be seen as much as possible all along the line. Later, when the general told him of his plan to appoint him chaplain, his answer was, "Do me the kindness of leaving me with the men. I am of more use in the ranks. I can do more good here."

He marched with the troops when they were moving camp, carrying his knapsack on his back as they did. Once a major, seeing that he looked tired, suggested that he put his pack on the wagon until the next halt. Teilhard shook his head. "A corporal doesn't set a bad example," he said.

He was popular with the men, but though he shared their hardships, they sensed the greatness of his soul and mind, and with his humility, an inborn dignity. They addressed him respectfully as Monsieur Teilhard, and they made makeshift altars for him when there was no parish church near. These altars were decorated with whatever was at hand. Sometimes a tap on an empty shell took the place of the bell. The regiment had no chaplain, and, since he was the only priest, Christians and non-Christians alike came to him for spiritual comfort. To the Muslims of the regiment he was the Sidi Marabout, or Revered Saint, a term they used for their own holy men. Though they considered all outside their religion infidels, when they lay wounded and dying they wanted him near.

Marguerite and her assistant, Mme. Parion, wrote, asking what he needed. He replied, mentioning such things as warm sweaters, woolly caps, and suspenders for the men who had none. Once during a lull he asked for a football. "No doubt you don't keep these in stock," he said, "but perhaps you won't have far to look for some generous person who will put up 15 francs which will buy an afternoon of occupation for the Eighth Tirailleurs." The two women delighted in sending him gifts, press clippings that would interest him, literary magazines, woolen socks to be distributed among the men. "I kept for myself the friendship with which it was filled," he wrote after receiving an especially welcome parcel.

The officers of the regiment held Father Teilhard in the same respect the enlisted men did. They broke tradition by disregarding rank and making friends with him. One Sunday night he said Mass in the colonel's cellar quarters and dined afterward with the officers. The next day he ate stew with the machine-gun sergeant-major. And he had many a meal with the troops, sitting on the ground and eating from a tin plate.

Soon after his arrival at the front he met Max and Jacques Bégouën, whose regiment was attached to the same Moroccan brigade as his own. The young men had caused a sensation among prehistorians two years earlier when they discovered clay models of bison in a cave on their father's estate. In the summer of 1915 Count Henri Bégouën received permission from the authorities to visit his sons at the Ypres front, and his meeting with Teilhard was the beginning of a warm and lasting friendship. In a letter to Marguerite, Teilhard described the father and sons as "men whom it is a delight to meet and live with, for we all share exactly the same tastes."

Teilhard's regiment was composed of assault troops and was moved from one end of the front to another. In battle after battle the troops fought, from Flanders to Verdun, from Dunkirk to the Marne. Under the fire of machine guns Father Teilhard and his men would dash out, or crawl unseen over the ground, to bring back the wounded.

At Verdun, during a particularly fierce battle, when every slope and ravine was bursting into smoke like a series of volcanoes, word came that the captain of the regiment was missing. The lieutenant-colonel called for volunteers to go out in search of him. Teilhard asked, as a special favor, to be allowed to go alone and spare the risk of other men. After some hesitation the officer agreed. Before dark he and Teilhard looked over the field and noted a spot, close to a German machine-gun post, where the captain might have fallen. At ten that night Teilhard crawled out on the field toward the German line. The next morning at dawn he could be seen returning, carrying the body of the captain on his back.

When the battle was over, Father Teilhard was able to say Mass for the first time in two weeks. There were so many to remember, comrades recently alive and in full health, now swiftly dead. And there were dangers safely avoided to give thanks for. "With the consciousness of the crying needs and bitter sorrows of the world, I said what was perhaps the most fervent Mass of my life," he wrote to Marguerite.

"We are all, Boche and Allies, floating downstream toward a cataract hidden from us by a bend, but whose roar we can hear," the Abbé Breuil said in a letter to him. "What will come next, we do not know. Civilization is in the melting pot again, but what the mold will be, we do not know."

Father Teilhard clung to his faith in man's continuing growth. Through the agony and heroism on both sides, the whole universe, ebbing and surging, was reaching upward with an almost heart-rending effort toward light and con-

sciousness, he said. The front was not simply the firing
line, an exposed area blighted by the conflict between
nations. "It is the 'front of the wave' carrying man toward
his final destiny. When you look at it during the night, lit
up by flares, after a day of more than usual activity, you
seem to feel that you're at the final boundary between
what has already been achieved and what is trying to
emerge."

In letters to his family he wrote little of the horrors of
war he witnessed and made light of his own dangers. As
during the peaceful years in Egypt, he described wild
flowers that were new to him and made drawings of them
for his father to identify. He told of water birds that were
of the same species but a little different from the ones that
flew over the Allier River. Just before an important attack,
when the tanks were already underway, he wrote, "We're
picking lilies-of-the-valley and mushrooms, and gathering
snails—what a rustic life!"

He expressed himself more freely to Marguerite. He
felt for her the same tender, concerned love he had for
Guiguite, and with it there was a communication of
minds. He described to her his emotions on the eve of a
battle as he made a tour of the trenches, offering communion to those who would accept it, feeling the clasp of a
hand in his, a hand that might soon be stilled in death. At
every battle he saw friends go over the top, with bayonet
and grenade, some never to return.

"What is going to emerge from this ghastly struggle?"
he wrote. "It is more and more the crisis, the desperate
slow evolution of a rebirth of Europe. Yet could things
move any more quickly? We must offer our existence to
God who neither wastes nor spoils, but rather makes use,
better than we could ever anticipate, of the struggle in

which we are enveloped. If I said I didn't feel any weari-
ness, I would not be speaking the truth."

In a moment of depression he remembered the time
just at the start of the war when he was helping Boule put
away the treasures of his collection where they would be
safe. He had felt buoyed up with a kind of triumphant joy,
handling, with such a direct physical contact, the fragility
of human hopes. He knew that, in spite of every disaster
and ruin, God's will was being attained. Even in its grim-
ness life was beautiful because he was convinced of the
transcendence of God.

From the beginning of earth's formation, potential life
had existed in the empty waters and barren land. And
there also was God, the source of all matter, of all the
elements of which life and the universe were composed.
Since the first molecule miraculously reproduced itself and
developed into a cell, then a cluster of cells from which all
living things were formed, there had been a reaching
upward, impelled, it would seem, by some conscious aim
that it would attain in spite of everything.

"Let the silent peace of your native mountains enter
into you and live in you," Pierre wrote to Marguerite as
she was leaving for a vacation in Auvergne. Nature lulls us
by its mask of imperturbability and gives repose to our
restless spirits, he said. The rhythm of change is too slow to
be seen in one brief life span. We see immobility, stability,
order, yet slowly and unseen we are borne along by the
whole past, in preparation for a world we will never know.

Once after a battle, when all was quiet, he went out
alone for a walk over the countryside. He saw the mist rise
up over the river, and a hillside stood out against the gold
and dappled sunset sky. The smell of the last gas attack
still lingered. In his mind he could hear again the whirring

sound, like a startled woodcock, of a falling bomb, and see it burst with sudden fleecy clouds shot with fire. And through it all the crickets had never ceased their chirping.

He felt a spiritual loneliness at times. As the regiment moved from place to place, he would come across a village church, damaged by shellfire or abandoned because the curé, the parish priest, had been called to war. He held services for the villagers and heard confessions. In parishes where there was still a curé he was asked to say high Mass and preach to the people. When other priests were stationed close by, the curé invited them all for a meal. It was good to be among them and forget, for a little while, an atmosphere that was stifling to the spirit.

In 1916 Father Teilhard began writing down his ideas in notebooks, whenever he could find the time. Sometimes he wrote while crouched in a trench, so weary his hands trembled as he formed the words. The same theme recurred again and again in all he wrote, that there was no separation between matter and the spirit, between the body and the soul.

"There is a communion with God, and a communion with the earth, and a communion with God through the earth," he wrote in the first of sixteen articles and stories produced during the war.

On the eve of the battle of Verdun, and during lulls in the fighting, he wrote three short stories expessing his thoughts through an imaginary soldier-priest. In one he saw the picture of Christ and the Sacred Heart, familiar to him from childhood, become transformed, radiating out into infinity until it encompassed the whole universe. Yet each object stood out separate and distinct in its individual character. In another story he pictured the Blessed Sacrament exposed in its monstrance, bright against a dark background. It seemed to expand, spreading with the murmuring sound of the rising tide, penetrating the heavens and the earth. Then it closed in on itself as a flower folds its petals, until it was again a small white object against a dark background. In the third story he wrote of the Host in the little pyx a priest carries with him. He tried to feel its presence penetrate his being until it and he became one, but he could not. "Each time I thought to have encompassed it I found that what I was holding was not the Host at all, but one or the other of a thousand entities which make up our lives: a suffering, a joy, a task, a friend to love or to console."

He wrote in a style that has been compared with the best of religious poetry, but these first writings were not approved for publication by the superiors of the Society of Jesus. They were not unsympathetic but, he was told, he had written of controversial matters and the general tone would have upset the quiet and cautious reader.

"Your article is intensely exciting and interesting to read," one of the censors said. "It is a canvas of thought covered with delightful images. But rather strong meat for our readers, who are gentle folk." A few days later another letter came from the same priest. He did not deny the difficulty of publishing papers on matters as Teilhard had treated them. At the same time he encouraged him to keep on writing and to try to integrate within Christian philosophy the results, suggestions, and interpretations that guided modern scientists.

"This impels me to classify more exactly my views on the reconciliation I glimpse between the passion of the earth and the passion of God on the meeting ground of human effort," Teilhard wrote to Marguerite.

A later article was accepted, but only after much editing. Teilhard would never have considered going over the heads of his superiors and submitting his writings elsewhere without their approval. He gave up the idea of publication and sent his articles to Marguerite or to Guiguite, who made copies to be circulated among his friends. There was nothing in his wartime papers that he was not to express more clearly later on. But at the time he asked himself in despair, "Will they ever listen to me?"

His ideas were too new at the time for some of the older superiors, who clung to a creed based on the limited knowledge of several centuries ago of man and the universe. They had been brought up in the belief that the world was created complete, never changing, the same now as it was in the beginning. "The mystical Christ has not yet attained his full growth, and therefore the same is true of the cosmic Christ," Father Teilhard had written. "Both of these are simultaneously in the state of being and of becoming. . . . Christ is the end point of the evolution, even the natural evolution of all beings. And therefore, evolution is holy."

In 1917 Pierre Teilhard returned to Sarcenat on a leave of absence. Two of his brothers, Gabriel and Olivier, were also at home on leave. A year later word came that Olivier had died of wounds received in battle.

After much discussion among the superiors, it was decided that the war could serve as Teilhard's tertianship. On May 26, 1918, he took his final vows. Seventeen years had passed since he had taken the first, simple vows of poverty, chastity, and obedience. Now, at thirty-seven, with a deeper understanding of their meaning, and without the slightest hesitation, he repeated the final vows. When he was asked in what frame of mind he took them, his answer was, "I am making a vow of poverty: never have I more clearly realized to what extent money can be a powerful means for the service and glorification of God. I am making a vow of chastity: never have I understood so well how a husband and wife complete each other in order better to advance toward God. I am making a vow of obedience: never have I better understood what liberation there is in God's service."

The following November Marguerite Teillard de Chambon made her own solemn vow to God to devote her life to education. On the advice of her cousin Pierre she made certain changes in the wording and added, "so long as it is manifestly the will of God to bind me to educational work."

Earlier that month the war, at long last, had come to an end. On November 8, 1918, Germany's Kaiser Wilhelm had abdicated and fled to Holland. An armistice was signed on November 11th, and at eleven o'clock in the morning the bugles sounded for "cease firing."

Pierre Teilhard was in the Vosges Mountains with his regiment, on the way to Germany's frontier on the Rhine. By the time they reached Strasbourg, French President Poincaré had arrived for the official return of Alsace to France. Streets would be renamed, the German language would be forbidden, and only French would be spoken and taught in the schools. For generations the Alsatians, living on the border between France and Germany, had gone through this change after every war between the two countries.

There were formal ceremonies in the morning, and in the afternoon the people had their own parade. They came from all the villages of the province, dressed in the costume of their region. The men wore wide black felt hats or caps of otter skin lined with green silk. The women had on their holiday aprons of bright colors. Some wore a wide silk bow for a headdress, others a tight-fitting bonnet with a starched, embroidered brim. They marched behind their mayors, wearing tricolored sashes, and the local bands, each with its own banner and emblem. Arm in arm they marched in a long, steady line that took an hour and a half to pass a given point. As Germans they were organized and disciplined, but underneath there was the spontaneous gaiety of the French. Now and then they broke into a rhythmic dance, with handkerchiefs waving.

Father Teilhard saw tears in the eyes of some of the most hardened soldiers as they looked on. In the evening all joined in a torchlight parade. The soldiers decorated their caps with oak leaves, and some wore the tricolor flag of France draped over their tunics. Pierre Teilhard marched arm in arm with a sergeant on one side and a warrant officer on the other.

His career as a soldier came to an end the following spring when he was demobilized at Clermont. Three times during his years of service he had received citations and medals for bravery, including the Croix de Guerre. After a visit with his family and a retreat at Lyons, Teilhard returned to Paris to continue his studies. He attended lectures in natural science at the Sorbonne and took up his work again under Boule. One day when Boule was showing a famous statesman and writer about the museum, they stopped before a display of the reconstructed bones of man's early ancestor. The visitor was impressed. "But what effect will this have on the religious belief of France?" he asked. Boule only smiled and pointed to the Jesuit, Father Teilhard, deeply absorbed in his work.

Less than a hundred years before no one would admit to a belief in the existence of man earlier than the few thousand years of recorded history. When the first skull of Neanderthal man was discovered in 1856, it was argued that it was of some deformed person of recent times. As for the chipped stone tools that were to be found everywhere, people believed they had been shaped accidentally. If cave paintings had been seen before the discovery at Altamira, they had not been considered worth recording. And the sea shells found on mountain tops were said to have been left by the great flood of Noah's time, or put there by the devil to tempt man into disbelief. As more discoveries were made, giving unmistakable evidence of the antiquity of life on earth, the division between science and religion widened, and there were bitter arguments on both sides.

Marcellin Boule's book *Fossil Man* was published in 1921. Teilhard reviewed it for the Jesuit magazine *Etudes*. Boule knew his subject well and presented it in a way that was proof against argument. He wrote of three types, or races, of man living at the same time, at the end of the last glacial epoch. This fact made it difficult to trace the origin of prehistoric man. Yet humanity formed one body with the earth on which it lived, a unity in its surroundings.

In his chapter of conclusions, expressing the power of this unity, Boule made statements Teilhard felt were unacceptable to religion without an explanation. "The letter of the Bible shows us the Creator forming the body of man from the earth," Teilhard wrote. He pointed out that a careful understanding makes one see that this earth was a substance slowly developed from the totality of things, that man was the result of the prolonged effort of "Earth" as a whole. "These ideas should not upset us. Gradually (though we cannot say exactly in what terms, but without the sacrifice of facts, whether revealed or definitely proved) agreement will be reached quite naturally between science and dogma in the burning field of human origins. In the meantime, let us take care not to reject the least ray of light from any side. Faith has need of all the truth."

No objection was made to the publication of Father Teilhard's articles on science, however liberal they were, but his best writings were still tucked away in his desk drawer, read only by his friends.

One spring afternoon, not long after his return to Paris, Teilhard called on Mlle. Leontine Zanta, a former teacher and now a close friend of Marguerite's. Mlle. Zanta's small salon was a meeting place for some of the most brilliant men and women of Paris, and also gifted young people starting out on their careers as writers or philosophers. Three other visitors were there that afternoon, including Mlle. Zanta's nephew, convalescing after the war. The other guests left after several hours of lively conversation, but Father Teilhard stayed on, enjoying a quiet talk with his hostess. She showed him a book, *The Possession of the World,* which was causing a sensation in Paris. Glancing through it Teilhard discovered the same ideas he had expressed in his wartime writings. It was encouraging to know that the present generation could become so excited over the subject of the divine in all things, yet he found himself comparing this book, which, though vague and carelessly written, had gone into four editions, with his own unpublished works. The thought came to him of a subject he had been wanting to write about for some time, something in praise of the spiritual power of matter. The author of *The Possession of the World* had made his readers feel that they were in touch with the divine. In his own work he would point out the struggle one must undergo to attain that touch.

In August, when he was in Jersey for a month of rest and retreat, the idea came to Teilhard to develop the subject as an allegory, writing it in a semi-poetic style. He began with a passage from the Bible: "And it came to pass, as they went on and talked, that, behold there appeared a chariot of fire, and parted them asunder; and Elijah went up by a whirlwind into heaven."

Elijah represented man. "The whirlwind, as you'll have realized, is matter, which draws with it and liberates those who know how to grasp its spiritual power," Teilhard explained to Marguerite.

In Teilhard's allegory the man lay prostrate, covering his face with his hands, and waited, as silent and still as the earth beneath him, when the whirlwind swooped down upon him. From a distance it had seemed no bigger than a child's hand, vibrant and quivering, playing aimlessly over the sand. Then suddenly, with the speed of an arrow, it came straight to the man, penetrating, with a breath of scorching air, into his soul. Now the tempest was inside the man. With both rapture and anguish he felt the sap of all living things flowing through him, infinitely gentle, infinitely brutal, a combination of all goodness and all evil.

There followed a dialogue between the whirlwind and the man. "Nothing is precious save what is yourself in others and others in yourself. In heaven, all things are but one. In heaven all is one."

The man remained prostrate with covered face as he listened to the words. It would have been easy, when the wind was gentle, to lose himself and become one with it. Then the wind became hostile and aggressive, and suddenly the man leapt to his feet and stood facing it.

"It was the soul of his entire race that had shuddered within him: an obscure memory of a first sudden awakening in the midst of beasts stronger, better-armed than he; a sad echo of the long struggle to tame the corn and master the fire; a rancorous dread of the maleficent forces of nature, a lust for knowledge and possession."

The man dug his feet into the ground and began to do battle. As they struggled, man against nature, the Voice continued to speak. "Son of earth, steep yourself in the sea of matter, bathe in its fiery waters, for it is the source of your life and your youthfulness.

"You thought you could do without it because the power of thought had been kindled in you? You hoped that the more thoroughly you rejected the tangible, the closer you would be to the spirit: that you would be more divine if you lived in the world of pure thought, or at least more angelic if you fled the corporeal? Well, you were like to have perished of hunger."

The long struggle ended and the man's eyes were opened to the ridiculous pretentiousness of human claims to order the life of the world, to impose upon it the dogmas, the standards, the conventions of man. He felt pity for those who take fright at the span of a century or whose love is bounded by the frontiers of a nation.

He saw God shining forth from the summit of the world of matter, whose waves were carrying up to him the world of spirit. And in the fiery chariot the man fell on his knees. There followed Father Teilhard's startling poem, *Hymn to Matter*.

"Blessed be you, harsh matter, barren soil, stubborn rock: you who yield only to violence, you who force us to work if we would eat.

"Blessed be you, perilous matter, violent sea, untameable passion: you who, unless we fetter you will devour us.

"Blessed be you, mighty matter, irresistible march of evolution, reality ever new-born; you who, by constantly shattering our mental categories, force us to go ever further and further in our pursuit of the truth."

Throughout the long poem matter is praised in all the effects it has on man, as it batters him, then dresses the wounds, resists and yields, wrecks and builds, shackles and liberates. It is the universal power uniting the countless cells that form life, bringing them all together, each in its individuality, until they converge on the way to the spirit.

Teilhard wrote to Marguerite from Jersey on August 8, 1919, saying that he had just finished "Elias." "Don't worry, that is not the title," he added. "I am fairly pleased with it, because I feel that in it I've got across what I was putting into words. But it will hardly be intelligible to anyone who isn't already familiar from other sources with my views of the role and nature of matter. Others, who have not been prepared for it, will take me for some sort of rebel."

August Valensin was in Jersey then, hard at work on an article concerning pantheism, and Pierre Charles came over from Belgium to join them. Both were impressed by this latest of Teilhard's work. Valensin wanted two copies to show to those in authority, to obtain permission for publication. Charles, whose influence was beginning to be felt at Louvain University in Belgium, also did everything he could to win over the censors, but without success.

Father Teilhard was prepared for this disappointment. "So it will again be something to be shown to friends," he had written earlier to Marguerite. "At any rate, I'll have put down on paper the basic core of what I have been feeling these last four months. That's always some satisfaction, isn't it?" He began work immediately on a purely scientific article entitled "Notes on the Structure of the Island of Jersey," and had the satisfaction of seeing it published the following year.

From the time of his return to Paris, Teilhard was busy working on his doctoral dissertation. This included more field trips, excavating sand pits in search of fossil teeth of Eocene mammals. There were days when he spent between seven and eight hours steadily digging until, when he arrived home at night, he had one idea only—to sleep. Boule had advised him to study some interesting material sent to the museum by a Rheims physician, as well as the fossils of Quercy.

In May 1921, two months before the dissertation was finished, Pierre Teilhard was made a Chevalier of the Legion of Honor at the request of his old regiment. The citation read: "An outstanding stretcher-bearer who, during four years of active service, was in every battle and engagement the regiment took part in, applying to remain in the ranks in order that he might be with the men, whose dangers and hardships he constantly shared."

Father Teilhard kept in touch with many of the friends he had made during the war. He was especially close to the Bégouën family, and visited them often at their Paris home, and when his studies were over he made a trip to their country estate in the mountains near Spain to see the caves where the clay bisons had been found.

Teilhard's oral examinations took place in March 1922, when he was called up to read aloud and defend his dissertation. Without hesitation the examining board granted Teilhard the title of doctor with very honorable mention. "M. Teilhard de Chardin is no newcomer to paleontology," said one of the examiners, who predicted a fine scientific future for him. At about this time Teilhard was honored with an award from the Geological Society of France.

Now that his studies were over, Teilhard again felt a longing for the East. He attended the Congress of Geologists in Brussels that summer and met a Chinese student, Wong Wen-hao, a co-director of the Chinese Geological Survey in Peking, who talked of the work being done in China in that field. But Teilhard was destined to remain in Paris for the time being. He was made assistant lecturer in paleontology and geology at the Catholic Institute there. These subjects were fairly new and the classes were not large, but Teilhard had such enthusiasm and knowledge of the subject that the students were reluctant for the lectures to end. Sometimes a class starting at five in the afternoon would go on until eight or nine o'clock.

Other Catholic colleges began inviting Father Teilhard to address their students. He spoke to them as both priest and scientist. He took his listeners back beyond the bounds of recorded history, to the depths of millions of years, and pointed out to them how life had been going forward in a given direction since its beginning. He explained also the importance of the individual in this continuing climb upward.

"At once humbled and ennobled by our discoveries, we are gradually coming to see ourselves as a part of vast and continuing processes; as though awakening from a dream, we are beginning to realize that our nobility consists in serving, like intelligent atoms, the work proceeding in the Universe. We have discovered that there is a Whole, of which we are the elements. We have found the world in our souls."

His notebook writings were being circulated among a growing number of people, and he found himself with a large following. His belief in the slow, steady progress of humanity brought a message of hope and confidence in the future, especially to the young clerics of France who, unlike their elders, could not deny the discoveries of science, yet, like their elders, wanted to keep to the faith of their religion. But the novelty of this belief, and the daring way Father Teilhard presented it, became more and more embarrassing to his superiors. The problem was solved in an unexpected way when Teilhard was invited to spend a year in China.

V
Arrival in China

AT ABOUT THE TIME Father Teilhard began his lectures at the Catholic Institute, an interesting collection of mammal fossils was sent to the museum for appraisal from northern China. Marcellin Boule turned the work over to Teilhard.

The fossils had been accidentally discovered by Emile Licent, a Jesuit priest from Tientsin, on one of his many geological expeditions. Teilhard wrote asking for more information, and a correspondence started between the two priests. Ten months later Licent urged Teilhard to come to China and join him in an expedition so he could see for himself the deposits where the fossils had been found. Teilhard's religious superiors gave their approval with an official assignment, and the Catholic Institute granted him a year's leave.

The Paris Museum agreed to finance the expedition,

which was to be called the French Paleontological Mission. Licent, who had been in China since 1914 and knew the country well, would be in charge of the expedition, with the understanding that the valuable finds would be sent to Paris and duplicates could be kept at the small museum Father Licent was establishing at the Jesuit College in Tientsin.

In February 1923, when all the arrangements had been made, Teilhard sent a brief telegram to Licent. "Coming for a year. Leave when?" Licent's reply was even shorter. "Arrive May 15."

Teilhard boarded the ship at Marseilles in the first week of April to start on his long journey east. Once more he passed the Straits of Bonifacio and saw the shores of Corsica and Sardinia. The ship glided on, beyond Sicily, then Alexandria, and entered the Gulf of Suez. Teilhard thought of his voyage to Egypt eighteen years before, when he had his first glimpse of the East. He tried to recapture the enthusiasm he had felt then, but at forty-two he wondered if this call to the East had come too late. He saw the jagged mountains of Egypt silhouetted against the setting sun like the teeth of a saw. To his left the granite and red sandstone peaks of Mt. Sinai loomed above the horizon, slowly disappearing in the fading light. He would have liked to climb those rocky slopes, not merely to test them with his hammer, but to find out if he, too, could hear the voice of the Burning Bush. But after all, he said, it was not in any one certain place, an empty desert or an inaccessible mountain top, that the Voice could be heard. The secret of the Universe would be revealed anywhere, to those who knew how to listen.

The ship made stops at Ceylon, Malaya, Saigon, and Hong Kong, long enough for only a quick look about the city streets. The tropical landscape, seen from a distance, was flamboyantly beautiful, with its lush forests, red and orange blossoms, and hills that dipped down to the very edge of the sea. But walking among the people, Teilhard saw a poverty and an apathy that appalled him.

Thoughts of Kipling's *Kim* kept coming back to him after his first glimpse of Ceylon. "The world is a great and terrible thing," the lama had said to Kim. The lama had been speaking of civilization, but it was the immense mass of undisciplined human power that overwhelmed Teilhard. He left the ship at Shanghai and made the rest of the journey to Tientsin by rail, with several changes of trains along the way. This brought him in close contact with the land and its people.

After forty-seven days of almost uninterrupted travel, Father Teilhard was weary and in a depressed mood when he reached his destination. He had seen so many types of men, with so many points of view, and at every level of human development, down to the most primitive. "My strongest impression at the moment is a confused one, that the human world (to look no further than that) is a huge and disparate thing, just about as coherent, at the moment, as the surface of a rough sea," he wrote to the Abbé Breuil three days after his arrival at Tientsin. He had come to China, following his star, to plunge himself into an unknown past, he said, but it was at a time when his thoughts were on the future, the ultimate goal toward which man had been striving since the beginning. He had looked upon the war, with its brutality, suffering, and heroism, as a wave carrying man on to a higher destiny. Could this incoherence of humanity also be a prelude to unification? "We must, at all cost, cling to a faith in *some* direction, and in *some* destination for all this restless human activity."

Within three weeks after his arrival, Teilhard and

Licent set out for inner Mongolia and the Ordos desert, a region enclosed within the great loop of the Yellow River. Licent, robust and active, was an excellent organizer. He knew just what to do in preparing for an expedition, taking into account all the things that might possibly happen.

The two priests made a good team. Licent had a collector's interest in the objects he found, but Teilhard searched deeper, looking for a clue to the past. He could determine the age of an object by studying the surrounding fossils and the strata of the earth. When he had looked over the collection at the Tientsin Museum, he saw that the tools Father Licent had brought back were of flint only. He decided to watch for carved and shaped pieces of stone, which would indicate an earlier race of man.

The first part of the journey was made by train, with a stop on the way at the wall-enclosed Mongol Blue City. There they made a formal call on the Mandarin who had command over the whole district they would travel. Licent presented a letter from the Geological Survey of Peking, and, after a ceremonial cup of tea, the Mandarin gave his permission for them to cross the Yellow River. He also provided a military escort of two armed soldiers.

At Pao-T'eo, the end of a primitive little railway line, Father Licent organized a caravan of ten mules, three donkeys, five muleteers, two servants, and the two soldiers.

"We are half like mandarins, half like soldiers, dressed in khaki and armed with several rifles," Teilhard wrote to his cousin. The depressed mood had left him in the excitement of preparation and the adventure of the journey itself.

The Chinese Republic was scarcely a dozen years old then. After imperial rule lasting over five thousand years, neither the people nor their leaders were ready for the change. Sun Yat-sen, who had been prominent in the over-throw of the weak and corrupt Manchu dynasty, served as president for only a few weeks before he was forced to resign. At the death of his successor the country fell under the rule of provincial war lords, each with his private army. The people were at the mercy of marauding soldiers and hordes of bandits.

Licent had earlier received letters from missionaries advising him against making the expedition. "The soldiers are still hostile," one wrote. "Recently a certain Colonel Feng said that the country will have to be rid of us, that we are to be killed and our heads hung on walls."

This warning, together with a severe drought, brought a change in the expedition's route. The first plan had been to cross the river at Pao-T'eo, on the north tip of the bend, and go directly to the banks of the Shara-Osso-Gol, at the southeast edge of the desert. Instead, the caravan took a roundabout course. They turned west and followed the whole great northern loop of the Yellow River, covering a large part of western Mongolia. Each new rumor of bandits close by brought another change of plans. Day after day, for six weeks, the caravan plodded over mountains and plains, circling their promised land, as had the children of Israel.

One evening as Father Teilhard was riding his mule, he looked to the right, out over the yellow Mongolian plateau, and to the pearl-blue hills beyond. Then he happened to turn left, and there, beyond the river, was another land, deep red and purple in the light of the setting sun. He had seen these desert colors often from the banks of the Nile, looking east toward the Red Sea. There, at last, was the Ordos.

"For two months we have never gone where we meant

to, and yet we have always found something," he wrote to Breuil in the latter part of July.

The caravan crossed the Yellow River at Ning-Sia-Fu, on the southwest corner of the bend, and headed east across the Ordos toward the opposite corner. From a camp-site forty miles from Ning-Sia-Fu, Teilhard and Licent went out to explore the region, as they had done at every stop. At the bottom of a cliff of wind-blown soil, along an ancient watercourse, they discovered a typical paleolithic hearth, a spot of earth charred by fires made 500,000 years ago. This was the first evidence discovered of Stone Age man's existence north of the Himalayas. The two priests made plans to explore further on the return journey, but now they were eager to push on. Teilhard was sure that the deposits at the Shara-Osso-Gol would form a link with the hearth site.

Several days later they reached their goal and pitched tents at the bottom of a canyon, two hundred and fifty feet deep, that had been carved through the centuries by the little river Shara-Osso-Gol. A friendly Mongol, with his large family, lived close by in a shelter scooped out of the earth beneath an overhanging cliff. He was intelligent and quick to understand why the two priests were digging. A separate site was opened for him and his five sons to work. The old patriarch kept an eye on the bronzed, long-haired youths, calling out directions from time to time. He carefully examined the fossils they extracted and put on one side the pieces of carved stone tools.

Another team of thirteen Chinese was hired, but they took little interest in the work beyond the wages they were earning. Mammal fossils had long been looked upon as dragon bones in China and were ground up to be used as medicine.

The canyon ran through a plain of steppes and sand-
hills, where wild gazelles grazed peacefully with sheep and
horses, and kites and cranes were almost as tame as household pets.

"I felt a pang of regret at leaving those wild riverbanks
where, after twenty-four days, we had adopted our own
free and easy ways," Teilhard wrote when they started on
the homeward journey August 24th.

The caravan moved slowly across the desert, with stops
for explorations along the way. A week was spent inside
the Great Wall, and ten days at the site of the paleolithic
hearth Teilhard and Licent had discovered in July. Since
that time they had found two more.

The caravan had grown to thirty animals carrying sixty
cases, weighing over six thousand pounds, of precious
material for the two museums. There were skeletons or
fossil fragments of animals long extinct in that region:
rhinoceros, a species of bison with enormous horns, deer
with curious antlers, hyena, and an ancient rodent. No
human remains had been found, but the three hearths
within a stretch of two hundred and twenty miles gave
proof that man had made fire and squatted close for
warmth, gnawing meat brought back from the hunt and
communicating with companions in chants and grunts. He
had left behind tools he had laboriously learned to carve
and sharpen, stone against stone. In the cases were several
hundred pounds of these tools, showing all degrees of
workmanship.

Father Teilhard thought of this expedition as a prelude. He was sure remains of early man would be found
somewhere beneath the earth and the curtain to the past
drawn back a little more.

At Ning-Sia-Fu the caravan was dismissed and the men
were given their wages. The two priests made the journey

from there to the railway terminus at Pao-T'eo on a heavy barge, following the current of the Yellow River. The cargo was carefully put on board and a tent was pitched on deck, with cots and camp chairs for two. The journey that had been so slow and laborious by mule was made in a week on the river. Father Teilhard used this time to write his impressions of the country while they were fresh in his mind.

It was autumn, his favorite season of the year. The sky was as cold and misty as an Auvergne sky, but the reeds were still green along the riverbanks. Swans and pelicans frolicked in the shallows, and now and then a flock of wild geese flew overhead, silhouetted black against the sunlight, as on a painted screen. Memories of other autumns came to Father Teilhard: autumns on the high plateau of Auvergne with Mont Doré in the distance, autumns in Egypt when the evening was almost cool as it settled over the violet desert, autumns at Hastings with the golden birches bowing to the wild sea wind. And now autumn in China, the China of desert and plains, of mud villages and lonely nomad tents, of child-like Mongolian herdsmen, seldom out of their boots and saddle, of pigtailed Chinese men, and women hobbling on tortured stumps of feet.

There was a slow fermenting in China at that time, with a gradual rise of leadership, but Father Teilhard, a newcomer to the country, saw only stagnation. What had happened to that desperate but splendid thrust upward made by the man whose remains lay hidden in the sands near the Shara-Osso-Gol? "I am a pilgrim of the futue on my way back from a journey made entirely in the past," he said. Once he had felt himself in the bow of a ship, watching the movement forward, but now he was in the stern, leaning over the wake and seeing the trace of what had passed. Yet, soon after his return to Tientsin, he declared in a letter to Mlle. Zanta, "I have a ferocious belief in progress of some kind, and I hold those who deny it as evildoers and heretics."

Throughout the expedition he had not missed a day reading his breviary, and following it with a few moments of meditation. At times he read in early morning while the animals were being loaded, or when he was jogging along on his mule, or in the evening after the work of digging and sorting was over. In August, on the day of Transfiguration, he had written the words of "Mass on the World," which he had repeated to himself for lack of any other Mass.

"Since once again, Lord—though not in the forests of Aisne, but in the steppes of Asia—I have neither bread nor wine nor altar, I will raise myself beyond these symbols, up to the pure majesty of the real itself. I, your priest, will make the whole earth my altar, and on it will offer you all the labors and sufferings of the world."

The prayer was long and fervid, to the Christ he worshiped, the "Christ of glory, hidden power struggling in the heart of matter, glowing center into which the unnumbered strands of the manifold are knit together. . . ."

Teilhard had expected to return to Paris at the end of the expedition, back to his work with Boule and the lectures at the Catholic Institute. But Licent, enthusiastic over their success, was making plans for another trip in the spring. Teilhard wrote to both Boule and the rector of the Catholic Institute, saying he would rather not remain too long in China, but he would leave the decision to them. Both men urged him to stay on for the second expedition.

The Jesuit College, called the School for Higher Studies, was in the area of foreign concessions outside Tientsin. There, away from the drab commercialism of the city itself, Father Teilhard found the peace he needed for writing and for laboratory work. The window of his room looked out on a wide vista of fields and marshes and freshwater ponds. With the abrupt coming of winter the ponds were frozen, but in May he had seen cormorants fishing there. He had to brace himself against an icy wind blowing down from Siberia as he walked across the grounds to the museum located in a wing of the school building. He and Licent sorted the sixty cases of specimens, scraped fossils, and made notes on them.

Often during that winter Teilhard made trips to Peking, where he found a cosmopolitan atmosphere that reminded him of Paris. The capital city was the center of culture for all China. Young Chinese scholars, educated in Europe and America, were returning with new ideas in science and sociology. And anthropologists, paleontologists, and geologists of many nationalities had been drawn there in the belief that it was in this part of the world that man's earliest ancestors would be found.

The remains of Java man, which had been kept locked in a strongbox in Holland for twenty-eight years, had only that year, 1923, been brought out and exhibited. When Eugene Dubois, a young Dutch doctor, first announced his discovery in 1894, there was as much discussion as there had been over Neanderthal man. Denunciations from the pulpit had been expected, but bitter criticism came also from the scientists. There had been much talk about the missing link, but this creature from Java, with his low, flat skull and a brain capacity slightly higher than that of an ape, was not the scientists' idea of the link between beast and man. Even the discovery of a thighbone, showing he had walked upright, failed to convince them.

Now another generation of scientists were examining Java man in a different light. A skull similar to his had been found in Australia three years before, and the search was on for others of his kind that would reveal a little more of man's development.

"It has been like a breath of fresh air to come back to the conversation of men who think and work as I do," Teilhard wrote during his first visit to Peking after the expedition.

At the January meeting of the Chinese Geological Society, both he and Licent read papers about their discoveries in the Ordos. The cordiality among the Chinese, English, Russian, Swedish, and American scientists impressed Teilhard. He renewed his friendship with Walter Granger, the paleontologist with the American Expedition in the Gobi desert, who had visited the Paris Museum on his way to China. At the French legation joking remarks had been made about the Americans, which Teilhard resented. "The more I see of them, the more I admire their ability to work and get things done, and the kinder and more approachable I find them," he wrote. "This is one of the discoveries that makes me bitterly hostile to 'accepted' judgements."

In addition to field trips and expeditions sponsored by the Smithsonian Institution and the American Museum of Natural History, the United States had helped establish the Peking Union Medical College and the Institute for Prehistoric Studies with funds from the Rockefeller and Carnegie foundations. Young Chinese scientists were being trained at both places to carry on the work.

Young Wong Wen-hao, the student Teilhard had met at the Geological Congress in Brussels, was back in Peking and had recently been made director of the Chinese Geological Survey, an organization of Chinese, Swedish, and American scientists. This was the beginning of a warm and lasting friendship. Wong's predecessor on the survey, Dr.

T. V. Ting, became another of Teilhard's close friends. Both men had discarded the western clothes they had worn in Europe and were dressed in the traditional long Chinese robe. Ting had studied at the University of Glasgow and had returned to China in 1912. As a professor at the Peking National University, he had gathered about him a group of young intellectuals, both scientists and rising political leaders. Teilhard had a glimpse of another side of China through them, a China seeking to regain its own identity after a long and humiliating European domination.

In early April, before the ice had melted along the riverbanks, Teilhard and Licent started out on their second expedition. It took the two priests north of Tientsin, circling the province of Jehol, in the southeast corner of the Mongolian steppes. Again there were rumors of bandits, and the local mandarins provided armed escorts to accompany them. A prolonged drought had caused a scarcity of water. In addition, there was a threat of war between Peking and Mukden, close to the region they planned to explore.

After traveling for twelve weeks, the expedition returned to Tientsin. No fine museum specimens had been found, but for Teilhard the trip had been worthwhile geologically. He had traced a sixty-mile chain of volcanoes about the same age as those of Auvergne. The fossils they had found were of animals scarcely known to that region, of the Miocene and Pliocene periods, dating back to the time, 12 to 15 million years before, when the great apes were first making their appearance.

Before returning to France Father Teilhard made a short excursion with George Barbour, a distinguished geologist from Scotland, then associated with the Americans in Peking. They explored the valley of Sang-kan-ho, a region around Kalgan, a few miles northwest of Peking. It was a puzzling area, the age of the formations was difficult to trace, and there had been conflicting findings. Since Teilhard did not expect to return to China, he urged Barbour to explore the region further before it was too late. There were only a few weeks left of the excavating season, and also this place, like so many parts of China, was threatened with civil war.

Soon after this excursion Father Teilhard left Peking for Shanghai to take the boat for France. While there he visited the grave of his sister Françoise. He thought of the ten years she had spent working for the poor in the city's slums, of how in the end she had given her life for China. He wondered if he, too, would be called to make this sacrifice.

A month after his arrival in Paris, in October 1924, Pierre Teilhard received a call to Lyons for an interview with his Provincial Superior. Two years before, he had written a paper, at the request of a colleague, giving his view of original sin. Somehow this paper had come into the hands of the authorities at Rome. Teilhard found his superior at Lyons friendly and sympathetic, but he was asked not to say or write anything more against the traditional position of the Church on the subject.

"At heart I am at perfect peace," Teilhard wrote that night. "Even this is a manifestation of our Lord and one of his operations, so why worry?"

He returned to his old room at the Paris Museum, at the foot of the stairs beneath Boule's office. There, at a long oak table, he worked on the fossils he had brought back from the Ordos. With books available and specimens in the museum for comparison, he could verify some of his earlier notes and make changes in others. The underlying red-earth deposits he had discovered were of an earlier period than he first thought. He now dated them back to the Eocene rather than the Pliocene era, a difference of about 40 million years. Licent kept in touch with him, telling him of the work he and George Barbour had done at the diggings near Kalgan. Also he wrote of plans for another expedition in the summer of 1926.

While Teilhard studied the fossils and bits of stone before him, he was searching deeper for a clue to the secret of life. Since the beginning of time, all life, including that of man, had existed in some form. He could see, during the long process, two sudden and mysterious thrusts forward. One was when, out of the elements, a living cell developed, the beginning of life on earth. The other was when thought and reason developed and man became a being apart from the animals.

He discussed these ideas with a few of his Catholic friends. One, Edouard Le Roy, a distinguished professor at the College of France, passed them on to his students, using Teilhard's word "noosphere," in comparison to biosphere, when speaking of life on earth with the power of reflective thought. Later Le Roy was to admit that in his books on evolution he had done little more than reproduce, sometimes almost literally, the result of their joint thinking. Teilhard was equally inspired and stimulated by his meetings and exchange of thoughts with Le Roy. "These Wednesday meetings have really become, for me, one of the best weekly 'spiritual exercises.' I always leave feeling better and fresher," he wrote to a friend. Le Roy gave him confidence, he explained in another letter. "He enlarged my mind and my feeling of loyalty to the Church."

Although Teilhard kept his promise and said nothing more in his lectures on his ideas of original sin, he managed to give four lectures on evolution. In talks to his students, to Catholic groups, and to young seminarians, and at a three-day retreat he held for lay students during Lent, he sensed the problems they faced. They were torn between centuries-old theological beliefs they had been taught and the reality of modern, scientific discoveries. Ideas for a book began taking shape in his mind at this time, and he brought them into his lectures.

"Teilhard preached to us his *Le milieu divine*," wrote Jacques Perret, one of the lay students who had taken part in the retreat. "The effect, on all of us, was enormous; here we found a brand of religious thought designed for Christians required professionally to live in the world and to do their work there."

Father Teilhard explained that work in the world was also part of God's great plan. He could be found in whatever one is called upon to do, as teacher, artist, clerk, or laborer. This message, to love God in all things, was written in the *Spiritual Exercises,* yet when Teilhard repeated it in his own words it was as if his listeners were hearing it for the first time. "For me, and for many of us, it was a great awakening," Jacques Perret wrote.

Before the end of the year Father Teilhard received another order from the General Superior at Rome. He must discontinue his teaching at the Catholic Institute and, furthermore, he must return to China. In despair Teilhard wrote to his friend August Valensin. "It is done. I am being moved from Paris, and the most I can hope for is to be left here for another six months to finish my work on hand, and get ready for the trip back to China with my friend Licent. My dear friend, help me a little—I've been keeping up appearances but inside me there is something like real agony, a real storm. . . . It is essential that I should show by my example that even though my ideas appear an innovation, they still make me as faithful as any man to the old attitude."

His friends in the Society of Jesus rallied around him. The rector of the Catholic Institute insisted on keeping him on the staff until the end of the school year. Even then he refused to take his name from the books, listing him as "professor on leave" instead. Though the future appeared dark, Pierre Charles told him, he should drown it in a brighter light. August Valensin joined him in a retreat that summer, and when Teilhard made another call on his provincial superior at Lyons, he found him affectionate and full of trust. By August the inner struggle was over and Father Teilhard again felt at peace, "without changing an iota of my views," he added.

"When I thought of the comfort I drew from the appreciation of all these minds, which were really reliable and devoted to the Church, I realized what enormous damage and scandal would have been caused by any act of indiscipline on my part," he wrote to Edouard Le Roy. "Nothing spiritual or divine can come to a Christian, or to one who has taken religious vows, except through the Church or his Order."

There were some who had urged Father Teilhard to leave the order of the Society of Jesus and become a secular priest, as his old friend and teacher Henri Bremond had done. Marcellin Boule thought he should defy the Church, give up the vocation entirely, and remain in Paris. He had earlier offered Teilhard a permanent position on the museum staff and hoped to make him his successor. "The faintest idea of a move to leave the Order has never crossed my mind," Teilhard said later. And to Valensin he wrote, "I am more and more determined henceforward to be *true*, without any compromise or diplomacy. If Our Lord is as great as we believe him to be, he will be able to guide my effort in such a way that there is no breaking point."

There would be other crises, with the same anguish and inner storm as in this one, when the breaking point seemed near. But when such feelings arose, he spoke of turning them, as best he could, into total sacrifice to God. "I dream," he said, "of seeing the Church really beautiful and beyond attack."

The following April Father Teilhard was on board the ship *Angkor*, bound for China. He settled down for the long voyage, reading, putting into shape the lecture on evolution he had given during the winter, and catching up with his correspondence.

"Air and sea: a thick living envelope, in which life swarms and hovers, as fluid and dense as the medium that holds it. Astonishment before the shape and the wonderful flight of the gull: how was that craft built? The worst failing of our minds is that we fail to see the really big problems simply because the forms in which they arise are right under our eyes. How many gulls have I seen, how many other people have seen them, without giving a thought to the mystery that accompanies their flight?

"May God grant it to me," he wrote to Marguerite, "always to hear, and to make others hear, the music of all things so vividly that we are swept away in rapture."

When the ship landed at Saigon, he took the little railway train to Hanoi to see something of the interior. For four hours of the six-hour trip the train passed through dense forest. Now and then Teilhard saw stretches of the forest being burned, and he thought of the tragedy of the destruction, the jungle swept away, the loss of magnificent wild animals, buffalo, elephant, tiger, deer, and peacock. Once he would have been inconsolable at the sight of this devastation, this conquest of man and his ally, fire, over nature. "Now I think I understand that we are witnessing the establishment of a new Zone of Life around the Earth, and that it would be absurd to regret the disappearance of an old envelope which *must* fall." This envelope included also the tribal life of the men who set the fires, picturesque, but belonging to a bygone age. "Temperamentally I am not disposed to think this way; it is through reflection and deliberation that I passionately welcome the life that is coming, without allowing myself to regret anything of the past."

Now he was eager to reach China and the work waiting there for him. A fellow passenger expressed surprise at the way Father Teilhard could sacrifice so lightheartedly the brilliant career that would have been his in Paris and accept exile in China. "But it is precisely there that the greatest progress is going to be made in the study of fossil man," Teilhard replied. "Some day his traces will be followed from Java all the way to Mongolia."

VI
Exile in China

"AS A GEOLOGIST, I really love this old land of China and all of gigantic Asia," Father Teilhard wrote to a friend at the end of his journey.

His first few days at Tientsin were spent making an inventory of the fossils Licent and Barbour had brought back from the valley of Sang-kan-ho, near Kalgan. They were older than the ones found in the Ordos, dating back to the old Pliestocene period, when man first made his appearance. There were no traces of man among them, but Teilhard was sure they would eventually be found in these deposits.

Before he and Licent started out on their summer expedition, Teilhard made a trip to Peking, where he found himself back in the circle of warm friends—Chinese, American, and European. Only Ting was missing. He had been made mayor of greater Shanghai, but he still kept in touch with Peking. A letter from him, touching in its cordiality and sincerity, was waiting for Teilhard when he arrived. The American Expedition, sponsored by the Museum of Natural History in New York, was in Peking in full force, since Mongolia was closed to them.

China was in a state of political confusion greater than before. Though there were signs of strong leadership emerging, capable of putting an end to the rule of war lords and bandits, the leaders were fighting among themselves. The ruler of Mukden, who had ambitions to establish another dynasty with himself as emperor, was supported by Japan. Russia supported the Chinese Communists. Sun Yat-sen, who had been restored to power with Russia's help, had died the year before. His successor, Chiang Kai-shek, now commander-in-chief of the revolutionary army, was building his forces toward a military dictatorship, also with Russia's support.

Teilhard and Licent set out on their expedition at the end of June. They had planned to be gone for three months, crossing central China as far as Lanchow, in the southwest corner of the Yellow River loop. The trip was a disappointment from the beginning. Their train was delayed ten hours in Peking due to a meeting there of two rival leaders and their armies and staff. Then, after an eighteen-hour journey on the train, they had to spend a week negotiating for muleteers and mules. The caravan had gone ninety miles when they found themselves in the firing line of a civil war. All roads to the west were closed, they were told, and there was nothing to do but turn back over the path they had come. They made a few detours into more accessible, but less interesting places and were back at Tientsin in August.

The two priests planned another expedition to the

valley of Sang-kan-ho, but the Kalgan region had also been fought over. Even after the place was cleared of soldiers, transportation was almost impossible. It was near the end of the digging season when Licent and Teilhard managed to make the trip in a borrowed mission car. Though they had only two weeks at the deposits, they brought back seven crates of fossils to work over during the winter.

"May God preserve in me the deep taste, and the sort of lucid ecstasy, that intoxicate me with the joy of Being—a joy drunk as though from an everlasting spring," Teilhard wrote to Mlle. Zanta after his return from Sang-kan-ho. "When I am immersed in rocks and fossils, I sometimes feel an indefinable bliss when I remember that I possess— in a total, incorruptible Element—the supreme Principle in which all subsists and comes to life."

In October the Crown Prince of Sweden, an ardent amateur archaeologist, visited Peking. At a meeting given in his honor by the Peking scientific societies, Father Teilhard made a talk in English. He was followed by Gunnar Andersson, head of Sweden's Geological Society, who was in China as Adviser for Mining to the Peking government. Andersson made the startling announcement that among the fossils sent to Uppsala University for study two human teeth had been discovered. They had come from a limestone quarry overlooking the village of Chou-Kou-Tien, a few miles south of Kalgan, and on the same stratum as Sang-kan-ho.

Eight years before, when Andersson was examining a small coal field a short distance from the quarry, he was impressed by the fossils he saw. On his next trip to China he brought two expert geologists, one from America and the other from Sweden, to explore the region with him. This time Andersson saw some pieces of white-veined quartz among the fallen debris. It was a kind of quartz not normally found around limestone. The stones had obviously been brought from elsewhere. "Ah, here is primitive man!" Andersson had exclaimed. "Now all we have to do is find him."

Andersson's announcement about the human teeth started the scientists of Peking on their search. Swedes, Chinese, Americans, and Teilhard de Chardin as the sole Frenchman worked together in friendly collaboration. There could be no digging until late spring, but they began their preparations by setting up the Cenozoic Research Laboratory, at the suggestion of Dr. Davidson Black, an American professor at the Peking Union Medical College. Black also enlisted the support of the Rockefeller Foundation for the enterprise.

The attention of scientists all over the world was now on Peking. A meeting of the Pan-Pacific scientists was held in Tokyo in November. When it was over, many of the delegates from Australia and New Zealand came to Peking. Alfred Lacroix, Father Teilhard's old geology teacher at the Paris Museum, and now permanent secretary of the French Academy of Sciences, was among the Europeans who had attended the meeting. He spent the month of December in Peking and Tientsin, and though by then his beard was white, he had lost none of his enthusiasm for exploring. He wanted to see the region around Kalgan, so Teilhard and Wong arranged for a trip there. It took fifteen hours each way to cover the forty miles, at temperatures below zero, in a run-down train with broken windows. Lacroix's special interest was volcanic rocks, and, with passports issued by the American consul, they went by rented car as far as the edge of the Gobi desert, twenty miles to the west.

When the last of the visiting scientists had left, Father Teilhard settled down to the tranquillity of his life at

Tientsin, writing and working at the museum. He had typed the article on evolution, written on shipboard the past spring, and it was ready to be sent off for approval. "I am not absolutely without hope that I may have it published in Louvain," he said. But this was not to be.

He was never to give up trying to convince his religious superiors that his beliefs were Christian beliefs and within the teachings of the Church. He went back to the subject of his lecture to the lay students in Paris, *le divine milieu,* and began work on the book he had planned. "I want to write it slowly, quietly—living it and meditating on it like a prayer," he said. He wanted to show how Christianity could and should infuse man's life with God.

"He awaits us every instant in our action, in the work of the moment. There is a sense in which he is at the tip of my pen, my spade, my brush, my needle—of my heart and of my thought. By pressing the stroke, the line, or the stitch, on which I am engaged, to its ultimate natural finish, I shall lay hold of that last end towards which my innermost will tends."

Soon after the New Year a letter came telling Teilhard that his connection with the Catholic Institute had been officially severed by the authorities at Rome, and that, over the protests of the rector, his name had been removed from the books. The news came as no surprise to Father Teilhard. "When I left Paris in April it was with the impression that my future was wholly uncertain, and I have lived in China with the growing feeling that in this country I have found a new home. So you see the break with my way of life from 1920 to 1926 was in some regards already complete."

At the same time it was necessary for him to keep his roots in Paris. He proposed to his superiors that he alternate between Tientsin and Paris, spending eighteen months at each place. If a point was made of it, he added, his formal residence could be Tientsin. And he would find the money himself for travel expenses.

The friends of Father Teilhard were more disturbed than he over this latest pronouncement from Rome. "If there is a God, as I believe, he will make the obstacles serve my progress; and in the end I will find myself more able than ever to make the light shine which some would like to see extinguished," he said. He had not been presenting a theory or system. He had instead tried to show the beauty, the pathos, and the unity of *being*. Those who looked for some narrow, logical system in his writings missed the great harmony of the Universe. "How I wish I could translate it into music!" he exclaimed.

At this time Teilhard also faced a break with Marcellin Boule. Since his return to China Teilhard had felt that the days were over when one came to the Far East in order to haul back everything to the West. Peking was fast becoming a scientific center, and the work that was being done there should benefit China as well as other parts of the world. He had continued to send valuable geological information to Paris, but there were fewer specimens for the museum's showcases. Boule's letter to Teilhard was affectionate, but he stated definitely that he was cutting off funds for the work in China.

Teilhard carefully considered his reply to Boule. He wrote one letter and destroyed it, knowing it would have brought out Boule's Auvergne temper. In his second letter he said the same thing but in a different way. A quarter of an hour's conversation would have set everything right, he felt. "I want to do everything I can to surround my old master, to whom I owe so much, with affection and respect," he confided to a friend. "But I will never put the museum before the general interests of human research."

Boule's decision did not interfere with plans for a spring expedition with Licent. Teilhard still considered himself a representative for the museum in China, and would continue sending in scientific reports. Alfred Lacroix, who had seen the work Teilhard was doing in China and understood his attitude toward it, offered some support. Another offer came from the Carnegie Foundation, on the recommendation of the American, Chinese, and Swedish scientists in Peking. Teilhard was asked to supervise the research and scientific work on fossil mammals found in China. It would be done through the Chinese Geological Survey, bringing him in association with Wong Wen-hao. This was work that Father Teilhard enjoyed, but his future was too uncertain for him to accept on a permanent basis.

The long awaited letter from Rome answering his proposal to divide his time between Tientsin and Paris did not arrive until April. The authorities saw no difficulty in his returning to Paris for a few months of scientific work, he was told, but there would be no teaching or lecturing. Father Teilhard saw a faint possibility of being allowed to remain in Paris if he confined himself to pure science. But for him that would be impossible. "Geology is like a root that pushes me up with its sap towards the human questions. . . . I cannot live outside that realm," he said. If it were not for friends in Europe and causes to defend, he felt he would rather not return. But there were friends and there were causes, and he made plans to leave for France at the end of summer, after the expedition with Licent, and come back to his new work in China.

Later that month Teilhard attended a farewell dinner in Peking for Gunnar Andersson, who was leaving for Sweden, and Sven Hedin, who would soon start out on an expedition to Turkestan. The host, Dr. Ting, had given up his political post in Shanghai and was back at his scientific work. Dr. Wong and two other Chinese were there. The Americans were George Barbour; Walter Granger, whose expedition to the Gobi had been called off; Dr. Grabau, a paleontologist who had been in China since 1920 and was the inspiration behind much of the work being carried on; and Dr. Davidson Black, Andersson's successor as supervisor of the excavations at Chou-Kou-Tien.

"I believe that never in all my life—family life included—have I spent hours so rich and cordial as that evening," Teilhard wrote. He felt, as he did on each visit to Peking, a sense of triumph at the overcoming of racial, national, and religious barriers. With it there was that special intimacy of friends on the eve of departure or at times of trouble. The table was strewn with apple blossoms, a symbol of transience. The guests made speeches of friendship and mutual aid, of glorious collaboration and of hopes for the future. Father Teilhard was reminded of the parable of the mustard seed. Two days later the group drove out to see the excavations that had already started at Chou-Kou-Tien, and they talked of the "Peking Lady," that prehistoric person whose remains they were seeking.

Licent and Teilhard had made their expedition to the mountainous regions of northwest China, where there was comparative calm after the uprisings of the year before. Only on the last stage of the journey had there been any trouble. They passed through a region the bandits had taken over, but by chance they met with a military convoy of a hundred soldiers and followed in its wake, unharmed. The trip had been for geological purposes, to study the structure of the region and map it. The collections they made were mostly specimens of lava, with a few fossils of plants and a kind of fish. The profusion of wild flowers they had seen, all blooming at the same time in the short northern summer, brought back thoughts of his native Auvergne to Father Teilhard. He longed to revisit the scenes of his childhood, yet, with the future so uncertain and shifting, as the time drew near for his departure he had the feeling of moving toward a great cloud. "But God also inhabits the clouds," he said. "And it is his trace that I come to seek."

He took the ship at Shanghai on August 27th, three weeks after his return from the expedition, and in October was back again with his family at Sarcenat and Murol. He also visited the country estate of the Teillard de Chambon family. There were hikes and automobile trips exploring the countryside with Marguerite, her two sisters, and Mlle. Zanta.

In Paris it was easy, as after each return, to slip back into his old way of life. He took up his work at the museum laboratory as if he had never been away, and his friendship with Marcellin Boule was as cordial as ever. Though he could no longer teach at the institute or give formal lectures, he had informal meetings with groups of students, and he held retreats where he spoke on such subjects as "Life and Matter" and "The Religious Value of the World."

To his surprise he discovered that he had become well known, not only through the scientific articles he had been permitted to publish, but also through the unpublished manuscripts passed from friend to friend. Letters that had come to him recently in Tientsin may have given some hint of this. Now in Paris he found himself with a following that had spread beyond his circle of friends and included believers and unbelievers alike. Young people were seeking, as he sought, for a more human Church. "I dream of a new Saint Francis or a new Saint Ignatius to come and give us the new type of Christian life (at once more involved in and more detached from the world) that we need," Teilhard had written earlier to Valensin.

Pierre Leroy, a young Jesuit studying for his degree, had been chosen by his superiors to work with Licent at the Tientsin Museum. He described his first meeting with Father Teilhard in 1928 at the Paris Museum. "His simple and natural greeting immediately put me at my ease. He offered me a chair while he sat casually on the edge of the table. His eyes, filled with intelligence and kindly understanding, his features, finely drawn and weathered by the winds of sea and desert, the glamour that surrounded his name, all made a deep impression on me." Teilhard talked to the young man for over an hour, telling him about China of the present time, and the promising future awaiting her. The young man listened also to stimulating ideas that were new to him. "From that moment we were friends; and so we were to remain until the end," he wrote.

The weekly meetings of Edouard Le Roy and Father Teilhard were resumed, with the usual exchange of ideas, each man stimulating and clarifying the thoughts of the other. Le Roy was working on a paper, soon to be published, about human origins and the evolution of intelligence. Teilhard wrote his comments, with helpful suggestions, on some of the pages.

In September Teilhard joined the Abbé Breuil at Count Bégouën's palatial country home near the Spanish border. It was a peaceful place in a setting of limestone hills, dotted with countless caves that were once occupied by prehistoric man. Breuil could stay only two days, but it was time enough for explorations during the day and quiet discussions in the evenings. "I have benefited by his wise advice," Teilhard wrote to Mlle. Zanta.

Bégouën had been detained in Paris and, after Breuil

left, Teilhard spent his time working on an essay on "the phenomenon of man" that had been going through his mind for some time. "The phenomenon of man" was what he called that extraordinary event, the emergence from among the primates of one species, man, capable of reflective thought. For 2 million of the earth's 600 million years, man has climbed up the dark road of the past, through all the various stages of his evolution, always advancing, yet always keeping within himself a part of all that he had been. "The stream of life has proven by its very success that it is irreversible," Teilhard wrote. "Why should it go back, since as a whole it has done nothing but grow since its beginnings."

The essay, of about a dozen pages, was finished before Teilhard's return to Paris. He sent it to his friend Pierre Charles in Belgium. Charles, now a distinguished theologian at the University of Louvain, was also one of the advisers on Jesuit publications. "I'd like to see the essay appear in the review *Scienta*," Teilhard said. "But I've no precise idea what sort of reaction reading them will have on people unfamiliar with the ideas I'm putting forward; I'm wondering if it all won't seem rather mad."

In November 1928 Teilhard left France, but instead of going directly to China he spent three months in French Somaliland. He and Pierre Lamare, a Jesuit geologist on his way to Yemen, were guests of Henri de Monfreid, a writer and adventurer Teilhard had met on his previous voyage to China. Monfreid, his wife, and their two small children lived in a large, airy house perched on the edge of the sea, with the waves beating against its walls. He had other property in Somaliland and Ethiopia, large estates in the hilly regions, and a power station and mill.

Teilhard and Lamare, with Monfreid as their guide,

explored the scorched desert, a plateau six thousand feet high, and valleys lush with coffee shrubs and banana and pawpaw trees. They were dressed as informally as their host in sandals, khaki trousers, shortsleeved shirts, and the kind of turban worn by the natives. For two weeks they sailed the Red Sea in a new boat Monfreid wanted to try out. At night they anchored under basalt cliffs, and civilization seemed far away. They cooked ground corn for their bread and the crew went out in a canoe to catch fish on the coral reefs—and when they could bought camel's milk or a kid to roast. One evening Monfreid's old servant, who had been with him through all his adventures, christened the boat by smearing kid's blood over the tiller, bows, and mast. Later in the night there came the smell of incense and the sound of voices chanting the Koran.

No two men could have been more different than Teilhard de Chardin and Henri de Monfreid. Teilhard's nickname for him was "the Pirate." But Monfreid, writing long after of those evenings under a starry sky when Teilhard opened his eyes to the presence of Christ in all creation and told of how all elements and all events were pushing upward, said: "From that time on, Teilhard was my brother." In humanity, in purity of soul, Teilhard, he said, was an extraordinary being. "Not a shadow ever disturbed his calm. He had the limpidity of a diamond, flooded with a divine light. The man himself was a light, surpassing measurement."

Though he was forty-eight, Father Teilhard explored coral reefs and mountainsides with the enthusiasm and energy of his student days. There were times when his companions were scarcely able to keep up with him. Once he insisted on entering a limestone cave in spite of an attack of wasps from an overhanging nest. His face was swollen and in pain the next morning, and though he was unable to smile, his eyes showed the satisfaction of discovery.

On their return from Ethiopia, when the train crossed a small viaduct, Teilhard looked down at the chasm below with a tiny little river running along the bottom. "If only the train could stop here! What a pity we can't get out and take a closer look!" he exclaimed. Just at that moment the little train gave a clank and jerked to a stop. It had gone off the track, and there was a delay of six hours to get it back on. Father Teilhard examined the layers of earth and identified their ages at his leisure. When they were at last on their way again, Pierre Lamare said, "Whatever you do, don't make any more wishes. However you stand with your superiors, you certainly know the right people in heaven. . . . [P]lease . . . [w]e've had our miracle for the day."

Teilhard sent fine collections of rocks to both Boule and Lacroix, along with observations he had made of that part of the world. As his visit drew to a close, he found himself reluctant, as always, to leave. "All this new country as I saw it with my friend de Monfreid immediately seemed home away from home to me, and I can't help wondering whether I won't end up by coming back here," he wrote. Then he added, "Yet oddly enough it doesn't stop me from feeling a sort of homesickness for Mongolia."

VII
Discovery at Chou-Kou-Tien

DURING THE TIME Teilhard had been away from China, the seat of government, under the Nationalist forces, had been moved from Peking to Nanking, some distance to the south. The name Peking, "Northern Capital," had been changed to Peiping, "northern city on the plain," but it still remained the center of culture. "The world and China can rock from one end to the other, while Peking remains unshaken under its blue sky, among its white flowers, and in the midst of its prodigious dust," Teilhard wrote.

He worked on the fossils that had been collected in the previous eighteen months at Chou-Kou-Tien. Another human tooth had been found, a lower left molar, which Davidson Black wore in a gold locket attached to his watch chain. Black had succeeded in enlisting the support of the

Rockefeller Foundation for his Cenozoic Research Laboratory, and it was formally launched in April 1929, a month
after Teilhard's return to China. C. C. Young, a Chinese
who had returned from studying in Munich the year
before, was assistant director and paleontologist. W. C. Pei,
a brilliant young graduate from the National University in
Peking, was put in charge of field work at Chou-Kou-Tien,
with another young Chinese, M. N. Bien, as his assistant.
They wanted Teilhard to join the group as official adviser
and collaborator.

Dr. Wong Wen-hao had moved to Nanking, where he
held an important government post, but he still kept in
touch with the work of the Geological Survey. He, too,
urged Teilhard to make the move to Peking and take on
the duties of scientific adviser for the survey. He was
already drawing up the formal papers in Nanking.

Was this just an unimportant sideturning he was step-
ping into, Father Teilhard wondered, or was it the main
road? His association with the Peking group so far had
been unofficial, but, with the wave of nationalism sweeping the country, he could foresee the time when a for-
eigner would find it impossible to do geological work in
China without an official connection with the government.
In early May, at Dr. Ting's urgent request, he went to
Chou-Kou-Tien with two Chinese geologists to study the
site. As a result, he was able to throw a little more light on
the history of what he felt would be a very celebrated site.
To be associated with the work done there was too important for him to think of refusing.

In the quarry, eighty feet of exposed hill slope was of
limestone with a network of fissures filled with red earth,
almost all containing fossils. The limestone was blasted,
and inch by inch the red earth was sifted and examined.
The puzzling part was to find that the fossils, though old,

were of the same geological age from top to bottom. Teilhard identified the age as the early Quaternary period, a million or so years earlier, a time when the earth of China was of red clay instead of the gray-yellow, wind-blown dust of the present day.

Father Bernard, the rector of Tientsin's College of Higher Studies and Father Teilhard's superior in China, approved of the move to Peking. He was planning a trip to France in the summer and promised to straighten things out with the superiors there. Now Teilhard felt that the only "dark spot is still good old Licent, whom I cannot just drop. Affection, gratitude, and prudence—in view of our common religious tie—all forbid it."

Teilhard made his last expedition with Licent from May 7th to June 10th. Their old cordial relationship was resumed as they shared the hardship of traveling in Chinese carts through deep mud and the excitement of exploring new places, of search and discovery. They went into Manchuria almost as far as Siberia and Teilhard was able, through his own observations and by comparing notes with a Russian geologist he met, to trace the relation of the structure of land in the extreme north with the parts of China he had explored earlier.

Ten days after his return to Manchuria, Teilhard was off to study the geology of the Yellow River basin with the Chinese geologist Dr. Young. They traveled with a six-mule caravan through parts of the country that had been closed to Teilhard and Licent in 1926, over the Shansi Mountains and the southern sands of the Ordos. For the first time in his travels, Teilhard was not made to feel an outsider. As an official of the Nanking government, with a Chinese scientist as a companion, he was cordially received by the authorities wherever he went. At the inns where they stopped for the night, everything was done to make them comfortable. Young, like Teilhard, was interested in studying the land itself, the enormous limestone mountains, the ancient red clay deposits, and the more recent yellow ones. They wandered from place to place with the caravan for three months. At the end of September, when they returned, Father Teilhard made his move to Peking. He took up residence with the Lazarist Fathers and spent his working hours in his office at the Geological Survey and at the Cenozoic Laboratory of the Peking Union Medical College with Davidson Black. The Jesuit House at Tientsin still remained home to him, a place to go for retreat and meditation or to write about spiritual matters.

As early as October there were signs of approaching winter in Peking. The leaves had fallen and water lilies were withering in the moats around the Imperial Palace. Ice had begun to form on puddles in the roads and the ground would soon be frozen. Father Teilhard joined Davidson Black, Wong Wen-hao, George Barbour, and C. C. Young for a last inspection of the Chou-Kou-Tien excavations before the work was closed for the season. By then more human teeth and fragments of human bones had been found. Young Pei was not ready to leave then. He asked permission to stay on and work a little longer, and this was granted.

Late in the evening of December 3rd, Pei arrived in Peking. He went straight to Black's office at the medical center, mysteriously holding in his arms a bundle of soiled clothes. From it he drew an object wrapped in burlap, which had been soaked with flour and water paste and dried. Inside the burlap was a well-preserved skull, with a cranium larger than that of an ape, which he had unearthed only the afternoon before. Here was Peking man, the object of seven years' painstaking search.

After working until the end of November and finding

nothing more of importance, Pei had paid his workers and dismissed them. Then he returned to the site for a last inspection, to measure for his report the amount of digging done. While probing through the sand with a measuring stick he uncovered the skull encased in rock. With hammer and chisel he worked alone, cutting the rock away from its surroundings. He then took the rock to his room, where he photographed it by time exposure with candle-light and prepared the wrappings to keep it intact. At dawn the next morning he hired a man with a jinricksha to take him the thirty miles to Peking. On the way they passed through an area where a local war was being fought, but Pei felt safe. If he were stopped and searched no one would suspect that in the bundle of soiled clothes beneath his long scholar's robe was a precious treasure.

For the first few weeks the discovery was kept a secret from all but the few scientists in Peking so that it could be studied in privacy. Unlike the high, rounded dome of Piltdown man, which Black as well as Teilhard had examined, this one was triangular, like that of the apes, though the brain capacity was larger. The brow was low and receding, with heavy bony ridges above the eyes. The jaw receded also, lacking a man-like chin, but the teeth were definitely human. The lower premolars were single-rooted, as they are in man, and the upper canines did not protrude and close scissors-like over the lower ones, as do those of the great apes. Peking man was older and more primitive than Neanderthal man. In appearance the skull resembled that of Java man.

The imagination was excited rather than satisfied with what had been found so far, Father Teilhard said. How far had this being developed? Had he reached the stage of reflective thought? Had he discovered fire or tools? It was not even certain that he walked upright, for no leg bones had been found, and it would be four months before digging could begin again at Chou-Kou-Tien. Roy Chapman Andrews, the American explorer, was in Peking that winter. When he was shown the skull he remarked: "He could not have been very impressive when he was alive, but dead and fossilized, he is awe-inspiring."

On December 28th telegrams were sent to the leading natural history museums telling of the discovery. Teilhard and Black together sent a message to Marcellin Boule. "New Year's Greetings. Recovered Chou-Kou-Tien uncrushed adult Sinanthropus skull entire except for face. Letter follows."

The news made headlines throughout the world. Five years earlier the newspapers had been filled with reports of a court trial in a small Tennessee town charging John T. Scopes with teaching the theory of evolution to his high school classes. The trial had been held to test a newly enacted state law prohibiting the teaching in a school or university supported by public funds any theory that denied the biblical story of the divine creation of man.

By a strange turn of fate, Father Teilhard, who had been barred from teaching in Paris because of his views on human evolution, had a part in one of the most important discoveries in the study of man's origins.

"Whatever we Christians may say on the subject of transformism or of any of the other general views that attract modern thought, let us never give the impression that we are afraid of something that may renew and enlarge our ideas of man and the universe," he wrote in an article about the discovery at Chou-Kou-Tien. "The world will never be vast enough, nor will humanity ever be strong enough to be worthy of Him who created them and incarnated Himself in them."

The finding of Peking man had been the result of close

teamwork, with scientists of various nationalities contributing each in his own field.

Davidson Black, as anatomist and anthropologist, worked on the skull alone. He was at his best in the late hours of night, when the halls of the building were deserted and there could be no interruptions. With dental instruments he drilled away the bed of stone that held the skull, grain by grain. After all the bones were loose he painstakingly assembled the skull back to its original shape and photographed it from every angle. Then he had a skilled pottery artist make plaster replicas and paint them to look like the actual skull. These replicas and copies of the photographs were sent to the American Museum of Natural History in New York and to the British Museum in London.

Father Teilhard's share of the work was in determining the age of Peking man through a study of the geology of the site and of the fossil animals found there—deer with jaws and skull bones so thick they appeared deformed, bison with triangular horns, a curious little dog, and a large tiger. A closer look at the site showed him that it was not, as he had supposed, an open fissure into which the bones had been washed by torrents, but the filled-in bottom of a cave more ancient than any yet discovered. The cave's roof had long been uncovered by erosion.

Teilhard made a short field trip to the Shanshi province, directly south of Chou-Kou-Tien, with George Barbour to verify his conclusion about the age of the region. Soon after Easter he went on another field trip with the geologist Young into northwest Manchuria, and in June he took part, for the first time, in an American expedition. He had received a cable from H. F. Osborn, director of the American Museum of Natural History, asking him to go along as prehistorian of the group. They traveled by automobile well into the Gobi desert, where they pitched their eight blue tents at the foot of a fossil-bearing cliff that was the base of operations. The Americans, with Roy Chapman Andrews as organizer, had been exploring this part of China for six years and knew how to save their energy. They were issued thick fur coats and fleece-lined sleeping bags, for the Mongolian winds were cold even in June and July. When the meat supply was low Andrews took his rifle and drove off, returning before long with a gazelle on the runningboard. Teilhard thoroughly enjoyed this expedition, and at the same time he was able to work out a connection between the geological structure of China and that of Mongolia. When he returned to Peking he learned that another human skull had been found at Chou-Kou-Tien. It was no more complete than the first one, but the shape was identical, showing Peking man to be a distinct type.

"The famous Sinanthropus skull is proving more and more to be a find of the first order—a solid fact that will be highly embarrassing to many out-of-date minds," Teilhard wrote to a friend.

The article he had written on the discovery of the first skull was published that summer in a French scientific journal, and another he wrote in collaboration with Dr. Young was published in Peking. But he was not satisfied with a purely scientific attitude about evolution. He saw a mystical side, of God "making man make himself." "No paleontological considerations can ever rival the dazzling greatness of the existence of present-day man," he said.

The essays Father Teilhard had written in France, "The Phenomenon of Man" and "What Should We Think of Transformism?" were returned to him marked by the censors with critical comments. During a peaceful retreat at Tientsin he worked on them, trying, as he would try all his life, to satisfy the authorities at Rome and still remain honest in the expression of his belief. He wondered about his little book of piety, *The Divine Milieu*. In July 1929 Pierre Charles had written from Louvain that it had been approved and was ready for the printers unless something unforeseen came up. A year had passed and nothing more was heard about it. And what had become of Edouard Le Roy and his book, *Problem of God,* he asked. "I'm rather worried," he wrote to a friend in Paris. "Another condemnation would do enormous harm to the current of thought our friend was beginning to canalize."

With the permission of his superiors, Father Teilhard returned to France in September for a stay of four months only. This time, instead of the interminably long sea voyage, he traveled on the Trans-Siberian Railway, a journey of two weeks. His return to China was by way of the United States, a country he had never seen before. His first impression of New York was of the order and majesty of the city, and the beauty of the skyscrapers, especially at night when their summits were lit up like lighthouses. Most of his time there was spent at the American Museum of Natural History, where he was warmly welcomed by H. F. Osborn. "An adopted son of the house," Osborn called him at one of two luncheons given in his honor. He saw Roy Chapman Andrews again, and others he had met in Peking, and he gave a talk in English to the museum staff. He was invited also to lecture to the geology students at Columbia University.

In a visit to Chicago, Father Teilhard stayed only long enough to visit the Field Museum. The founder's grandson, Henry Field, accompanied him, then had him to dinner at his home before seeing him off at the railway station. Teilhard took the southern route to San Francico so he could at least have a glimpse of the American desert.

He passed within a tempting sixty miles of the Grand Canyon, but his time was limited and he wanted to have a few days in San Francisco before his ship sailed. That city was like a giant Riviera to him, with the Pacific as its Mediterranean. At the University of California Teilhard made new friends and was as cordially received as at the American Museum of Natural History in New York. In France one could scarcely imagine such a university as this one, he said, with hundreds of students living the way we associate with the Greeks, bursting with health in the glorious sunshine. At first glance those husky, athletic youths would seem to care nothing for learning, but in his own field he found several keen young workers.

"I realize I did well to return to Peking through the United States," Teilhard wrote to the Abbé Breuil. "If I were only forty!" He was sure that if for any reason Peking should fall through, he could find a home in America and work in his own field waiting for him.

A few weeks after his return to China Father Teilhard started out on the longest and most hazardous of all his expeditions. He had been asked in 1929 to take part in the Citroën Central Asian Expedition, later to be known as the great Yellow Expedition. It was organized by the Citroën Motor Company of France to prove the adaptability of their equipment over uncharted territory, and also to trace the old silk route for possible land communication between the East and the West. The expedition was to be divided into two groups. One, starting from Beirut and crossing the Himalayas, would be led by Georges-Marie Haardt, who had taken an earlier expedition across the Sahara. The China group, led by Victor Point, a French naval lieutenant, would start from Peking and cross the whole of China to the meeting place, Kashgar, close to the Russian border in Chinese Turkestan.

Though the expedition seemed more a commercial than a scientific undertaking, Father Teilhard, after a meeting with Point in Peking, had agreed to take part. It would give him the opportunity he had been wanting to study the geology of a vast and almost unexplored region.

Two years had gone into the preparation of the expedition. The National Geographic Society in Washington, recognizing its scientific possibilities, helped finance it with a sum of money equal to that given to Admiral Byrd for his South Pole expedition. Haardt enlisted engineers and a staff of mechanics, a doctor for each of the two groups, a cameraman, a painter, and a writer to record the history of the journey. In addition, Generalissimo Chiang Kai-shek, hostile to foreign expeditions, had insisted on having representatives of the Chinese Nationalists included.

The China convoy broke down ninety miles from Peking. The rubber of the caterpillar tracks collapsed and new ones had to be sent by way of Siberia. This meant a delay of several weeks. Father Teilhard went to Tientsin for a retreat during Holy Week. While there he saw Licent's new assistant, Pierre Leroy, the young Jesuit he had met in Paris three years before. Leroy accompanied Teilhard on his return to Peking and was shown around the Cenozoic Laboratory. Teilhard asked Pei if anything new had turned up at Chou-Kou-Tien. Pei opened a drawer and took out a piece of quartzite. Teilhard examined it and saw that it had been crudely but certainly shaped by hand.

"This is very important," he said, and he asked exactly where it had been found. Soon he made a tour of the excavations himself, and after an hour of searching he found more worked stones and blackened objects such as a bison horn and ostrich egg shells. Peking man, some one or two million years before, had made tools and built fire. He had passed beyond that mysterious boundary that separates reflection from instinct, man from animal, noosphere from biosphere. "Once the light begins to shine, it spreads everywhere," Father Teilhard said.

Both he and Black were eager to have the Abbé Breuil come to China to examine and appraise the findings. Arrangements were made for him to arrive in early autumn, when Teilhard expected to be back from the expedition and before the excavation was closed for the winter.

By the middle of May the China convoy was ready to start on its way. "Climbing on to the caterpillar as though I were mounting a camel, I asked only one thing of the expedition, to take me across Asia," Teilhard wrote to his brother Joseph. The huge trucks and tractors headed due west toward their goal, the far distant border of China. Through snowstorms and sandstorms and under cloudless blue skies they lumbered over a wild and desolate land, corrugated by cliffs and ravines. Sometimes a truck sank deep in the desert sand, and all worked together, digging and pushing, to get it out. Sometimes a motor stalled, and while the mechanics were repairing it, Father Teilhard went out exploring with his geologist's hammer and magnifying glass. Once the convoy came to the edge of a sheer drop and the vehicles had to back out, one after the other, and chart another course.

After a month of travel, covering seven hundred and fifty miles, they stopped for several days to give the motors a rest and renew the strength of the men. At this point the Chinese Nationalists, surly and suspicious from the beginning, demanded equal control of the expedition. A peaceful settlement was arranged, through the diplomacy of

Father Teilhard acting as an official of the Chinese survey, and an agreement was signed by both sides.

After a rest of ten days the convoy continued on its way. A week later they reached the Hami oasis, across the border of Sinkiang. Sounds of gunfire could be heard from a village ahead, then there was a sudden silence as the trucks came near. A battle had just been fought between the eastern Turks and the Chinese. Chinese flags and regimental colors were being raised, and Chinese riflemen were holding the ridges. There was devastation in the village. Corpses were lying on the roadside, children hid in terror under overturned carts. A woman was weeping beside her dying husband. Tethered animals were tugging wildly at their ropes and halters.

"Have you a doctor?" someone called out.

Delastre, the doctor, was already setting up an aid post with the help of Father Teilhard. Soon they were surrounded by the wounded, but the lead bullets of the Turks had taken their toll.

The convoy moved on toward Urumchi, the capital of Sinkiang. This was the last lap of the journey out, and the men no longer felt that Kashgar, the meeting place of the two groups, was only a dream. Teilhard found his work more and more absorbing. "I am in the heart of one of the most mysterious and sacred of geological regions, and I think I am finding the key to it by establishing step by step its connection with eastern China," he wrote. The formations and structures showed a greater coherence than he had hoped to find and this knowledge, he felt, would help in his future work. But he had discovered no fossils and nothing in the way of prehistory.

A little over two months after leaving Peking, the group arrived at Urumchi, and there they were held.

Marshall King, the sly, despotic ruler of Chinese Turkestan, refused permission for them to advance further. The
men were installed in a pagoda surrounded by stately trees,
with a view of the snow-covered mountains to the west.
They were well treated and everything was done for them,
but they were prisoners, kept there from the middle of
July until the middle of December. By the end of August
the war lord was persuaded to allow Haardt and his group
to join them at Sinkiang. No more than four of the vehicles and only a few of the men could go to meet Haardt's
party. Father Teilhard was one of the men selected by
Point to accompany him.

For two weeks the caterpillars took them over a route
no truck could ever make, through rocky passes, marshes,
rivers, and sands. After traveling seven hundred miles the
group reached Aksu, where they stopped to wait, for word
had come that Haardt had already left Kashgar and was on
his way.

The cold of autumn had already set in at Urumchi,
north of the mountains, but Aksu was sunny and warm.
Teilhard and his companions were guests of a merchant
and the days of waiting were a pleasant interlude. Ripe
bunches of grapes hung from the pergola of the merchant's
garden, and the peach and apple trees were weighed down
with fruit. There were no Chinese in this part of Turkestan, except a few government officials and merchants. The
place had an atmosphere of the Middle East, with Afghans,
Persians, and Hindus, the men bearded and turbaned and
the women veiled. At evening there could be heard from
every side the chant of muezzins calling the faithful to
prayer.

Father Teilhard was fishing at a stream by the side of
the road one day when a cloud of dust rose over the
horizon. Soon he saw the western group of the expedition

approaching. He dropped his rod and rushed forward. "So you're here at last. We've had a rather long wait for you, you know," he teased. "Father! My good friend, my dear friend," Haardt exclaimed, embracing him.

The joy of reunion did not last long. Back at Urumchi they were still kept prisoners. The smooth-talking Marshall King provided all the men with living quarters in heated houses and comfortable Mongol tents, and there were parties and entertainment for them. But it took Haardt two months of negotiations before they were allowed to leave.

"Breuil must have gone through Peking at the end of October, just in time to appraise and criticize the finds of tools which I started last April," Teilhard wrote to his cousin. "And to think that I was not there to receive my old friend after I had induced him to come!"

The journey back to Peking was one of extreme hardship. The cold was so intense that the vehicles had to push on over the unmapped wasteland twenty hours out of the twenty-four. If they stopped long the radiators would freeze, and if they kept the motors running they would waste precious fuel. Twice a day there was a pause for a meal. The men, so bundled in furs they could scarcely move, ate standing up. The soup, boiling hot when it was ladled into the metal bowls, became an icy mush before it was all eaten. The exhaustion was worse even than the cold, for it brought on a dangerous lethargy. Father Teilhard spoke of this experience as the hardest and most rewarding of his career. "We missed many opportunities; we were too much at the mercy of our machines; but what a compensation for me that I have now seen with my own eyes the vast zone that lies between Kashgar and Tsitsikar."

They spent New Year's day at a mission along the way. Though there was not a practicing Christian among the men, when Father Teilhard celebrated Mass everyone attended.

"So may success crown our enterprises. So may joy dwell in our hearts and all around us. So may what sorrow cannot be spared us be transfigured into a finer joy, the joy of knowing that we have occupied each his own station in the universe, and that, in that station, we have done as we ought.

"Around us and in us, God, through his deep-reaching power, can bring this about. And it is in order that he may indeed do so that, for all of you, I am about to offer him this Mass, the highest form of Christian prayer."

André Sauvage, the expedition's photographer, wrote of Father Teilhard: "There was something very handsome about him. . . . He had the matchless style of an unobtrusive, yet irresistible distinction. There was nothing obtrusively clerical about him; in gesture and deportment he was as simple as could be. He was gracious and obliging, yet as unyielding as a stone wall."

The young naturalist of the expedition, looking back on the adventure long afterward, wrote: "Teilhard—you'd have to have seen him in those days! And I wish that you had seen him, or could see him standing before you as I do, in memory: vibrant as a flag fluttering under the Asian sky, energetic, lively, generous, tireless, greeting each day with a burst of joyous enthusiasm—one minute running like a youngster for a hammer to check something, sparing willing workers almost as little as himself."

After reaching Peking Haardt tried to persuade Teilhard to continue with the expedition on to Indochina. The hardships were over and the rest of the journey would be something of a holiday. It was for this reason that Teilhard refused. When the men had left Peking he went to Tientsin for an eight-day retreat, "so as to get possession over my inner self again," he said. When the expedition had reached Peking on February 12th, he learned that his father had died only the day before. There was also the news that three of Edouard Le Roy's books and the second volume of a fourth had been put on the Index of Forbidden Books and Le Roy had been forced to make a recantation. It was only because Father Teilhard's own Order had come to his defense that he was not caught in the backwash of the affair. There was even some hope that his *The Divine Milieu* would be approved for publication if he agreed to make some changes.

On March 18th, after he had returned to his work at the Cenozoic Laboratory, Teilhard received word that Georges-Marie Haardt had died of pneumonia in Hong Kong. The expedition, which had started out with such a flourish, was brought to a sudden end. "I imagine that had Haardt been able to foresee his end, he would have appreciated there was something fine in being struck down by death in the full vigor of activity," Teilhard said. But the desert would have been a nobler tomb for him, he added. He regretted now that he had not gone on with the expedition, and missed being with Haardt in his last moments. "From what I knew of him, he would have turned to me for support and I am sure that I could have eased his passing."

VIII
Expeditions to India, Java, and Burma

THE FOLLOWING SEPTEMBER Father Teilhard returned to France for a stay of four months. His friends were trying to have him established in Paris permanently, but again the superiors of his Order in Rome were worried about his outspoken lectures. His Provincial Superior urged him to use more caution in what he said and wrote. "So one can no longer even speak of things which are only distantly relevant to religion, and Christians are beginning to find this situation quite normal," Teilhard wrote to Valensin after hearing of another Catholic writer whose works had been censored. "Soon we shall ask for nothing better than the regime that the Gospel came to break two thousand years ago."

At the end of January, Teilhard was on his way back to China. For the first ten days of the voyage he was accompanied by the Abbé Breuil, who was making a visit to French Somaliland. Breuil was, as usual, gay and vivacious, "at the top of his form," Teilhard wrote to Bégouën. At Jibuti, Monfreid, looking more than ever like a pirate, drew alongside the ship in his dhow, with his Somali boatmen, to take Breuil on board, while the ship's passengers looked on in delight. "I felt a great gap when he left," Teilhard said. "I hope indeed that it will be good hunting for Breuil."

Two months after his return to Peking, Teilhard received a message from Rome instructing him to refuse any offer of a position or official appointment in Paris. He accepted this without the despair he had felt in 1925. What was needed was not revolt, but more love, he felt. "There is only one course open to me: to develop what I believe more intensively than ever, and mingle more intimately than ever with the blood I dream of correcting."

In July he went with Black and Grabau to attend a meeting in Washington of the International Geological Congress. At the end of a ten-day session Teilhard and George Barbour joined a group on an exploration trip across the country. They had three private railway cars, a pullman, a baggage car, and a car rebuilt as a laboratory and conference room. The cars were pulled off to a siding during the day while the scientists made field trips. At night these same cars were coupled to one or another of a series of trains, and they were on their way.

Again Teilhard was impressed, as on his first trip to America, with the freshness and expansiveness of the country. Here he breathed an atmosphere that was lacking in France. He felt especially at home in California, where he spent a month. "I am exceedingly fond of these wild, sun-drenched mountains, covered with ilex and laurel, or with cactus and yucca. And then, life is so simple, so unconventional! You sleep in the open, eat whenever you feel inclined, perched on a high stool at a counter. Nobody bothers you if you want to be alone."

In the laboratory of the University of California at Berkeley he observed a team of bright young research men at work. And he studied the geological structure of the high Sierras, the Yosemite, and down the coast as far as Santa Barbara, comparing it with China, on the opposite side of the Pacific.

It was Father Teilhard's custom, after returning to China, to spend a week in retreat at Tientsin, to get hold of himself spiritually and intellectually. By the middle of October he was back in Peking and at Chou-Kou-Tien. Before the excavation season ended, another cave was uncovered. It was of a later period, showing traces of an upper paleolithic culture, with two human skulls, tools of stone and bone, necklaces of pierced foxes' teeth, and fossil remains of animals of that period. And on a lower level there were fossils proving that this had been the home of baboons before the appearance of man. "What a menagerie! What a hotel!" Teilhard exclaimed.

He and Black saw the need of correlating the Chou-Kou-Tien site with other places where evidences of prehistoric man had been found. Teilhard was familiar with the geology of northern China, and now they talked of expeditions through the central and southern parts of the country and beyond.

At the meeting in Washington the most exciting topic of discussion had been the finding of Peking man. Since the news was first made public, searches were on in other parts of Asia, for it was believed that man had originated in this part of the world. A young German scientist, Helmut de Terra, had been exploring India and the

Himalayas, under the sponsorship of American organizations. He gave a talk on the affinities between the Alps and the Himalayas, and he told of finding Stone Age tools around Kashmir and the Himalayan foothills. Both Teilhard and Black were very much interested and wanted to know more.

Davidson Black was climbing around the hills of Chou-Kou-Tien one day in January when he suffered a mild heart attack. He was put in the hospital for five weeks of examination and rest. While there he drew up plans for expeditions during the next two years. He had spoken to George Barbour in Washington about coming to China to join Teilhard in a study of the Yangtze River basin. Now he wrote a letter giving more of the details. He also wrote to Helmut de Terra, which resulted in de Terra's invitation to Teilhard to take part in an expedition to northern India he was planning for the autumn of 1935. On March 17th Black felt able to return to his work. He was in high spirits and full of plans for projects as he stopped to talk with his colleagues, then he went to his laboratory alone. A few minutes later he was found dead.

Davidson Black would be hard to replace, as a scientist and as a friend. Teilhard was asked to take on the work of directing the Cenozoic Laboratory until a successor to Black could be found. It seemed strange to be sitting at his friend's desk, writing with pencils that "Davy" had sharpened. "He was the companion of my mind and my heart," Teilhard said. Weeks later he wrote, "Missing him is like a shadow, or an emptiness that I carry with me wherever I go."

Dr. Ting had given up science to return to public life in Nanking. Wong was in the hospital in serious condition after an automobile accident. Except for the younger scientists C. C. Young and Pei, Teilhard was left to carry on Black's unfinished work alone.

George Barbour was on his way to China when Black died. Teilhard and Young were waiting for him when his ship docked at Shanghai. After they gave him the news, the three sat together over a meal at the hotel, discussing their next step. It was agreed they would carry out the expedition as it had been planned, tying together the basins of the Yangtze and the Yellow rivers. By making a thorough study of the geological stages of evolution in central China and comparing it with what they already knew of the northern part, by searching for evidences of glaciation and examining animal fossils, they hoped to fix more accurately the age of Peking man and to learn something about his ecological surroundings, the geography, climate, and the kind of food he was able to find.

They set out on their expedition at the end of March, traveling for four and a half months by steamboat and sampan, in palanquin, automobile, and plane, and at times on foot. The trip was broken in May so that the men could take part in a memorial service for Davidson Black. Teilhard again went to Tientsin for a retreat, then came back to spend three days with Barbour at Chou-Kou-Tien examining the latest findings. For the second part of their journey they started out from Hankow and made the ascent on the Upper Yangtze all the way to the foothills of Tibet. Their last month was spent in Honan, bordering the lower bend of the Yellow River. The province had now been cleared of bandits and for the first time in a generation geologists were able to explore and study it.

Father Teilhard often spoke of his outward and his inward self. Outwardly he was intent on his scientific studies, whether in the field, the office, or the laboratory, but there was a time set aside each day for prayer and meditation and for his philosophical writings. George Barbour described the expeditions he made with Teilhard, their travels and observations by day, and the stops at night, under tents or in mission guest houses or Chinese inns. After the evening meal they worked on their field notes, compared conclusions, and made plans for the next day. Then they set up their folding cots and blew out the light, which had been attracting mosquitoes. "With the work of the day behind him, Teilhard would talk of the ideas nearest his heart," Barbour wrote. He spoke of the villagers they had seen, living at starvation level and crowded too close together, plagued first by drought and then by flood.

"The world is getting too full, and, with people living shoulder to shoulder, we *must* find a new way to settle our differences without coming to blows to get what we need," Teilhard said.

"Yes, it always seems to come back to material things in the end—money, stone axes or whatnot, with which to 'buy' what we think our bodies feel they cannot do without," Barbour answered.

"But don't you think that if we are less selfish, we might feel the other man's needs also, and live peaceably with him in love, and perhaps rise to a higher level of spiritual life as a result? I am coming to feel that this is *the* key to the problems of the nations of the world. The Communists see only the material needs of people, and push forward to improve the living conditions of the masses. But they do not see the importance of the individual's need for upward spiritual growth. And perhaps men of the Church do not always feel the hunger and physical pain which these farmers endure just to stay alive.

Surely the path of future development must be the re-
sultant of progress in two directions—forward and
upward."

"Or it might be a spiral, like a road up a mountain in a
mist."

"I agree," said Teilhard, "provided you continue to
seek the summit."

The expedition came to an end in August, and Teilhard took up his work at the Geological Survey and the
Peking Union Medical College. There were also reports to
write on the season's findings at Chou-Kou-Tien and on
the specimens he and Barbour had brought back. That
winter, he declared, was the busiest and most interesting in
his scientific life. During the day he plunged himself back
into the remote past, reading signs of an awakening intelligence in early man through the tools he made and used,
and, through the fossil animals and charred bones in his
cave, seeing clues to a way of life long forgotten.

In the evening, back in his room in the house of the
Lazarist Fathers, Teilhard's thoughts were turned to a
future equally remote. "The past has revealed to me how
the future is built," he said. At fifty-four, he still felt as he
had when he was young, that there was something immense, something beautiful about to take place throughout the world. "And we must abandon ourselves to the
mighty current of this development."

There would come a time, he said, when, as a result of
the laborious search carried on throughout the world in
ancient caves and gravel riverbeds, the pattern of history
would fit together. "But for those who come a long time
after us these facts whose attainment cost us so much will
be accepted on an equal footing with our acceptance of the
alphabet or the secret of the stars."

"And it will then be the season for a march *entirely*

forward," he wrote that winter at the end of an essay entitled "The Discovery of the Past." "Then at last man will
have understood the essential word whispered to him by
the ruins, the fossils, and the ashes, 'The only thing worth
the trouble of finding is what has never yet existed.' The
only task worthy of our efforts is to construct the future."

In another essay, "Why I Believe," written that year at
the request of a Jesuit publication, he explained his religious beliefs with such frankness that before he was
through he knew that this, too, would be disapproved for
publication. "In that case there is always private circula-
tion," he said. Again and again he would point out the
need for religion to keep up with the advance of science.
"If our humanity is really to become more adult than it
was two thousand years ago, it somehow needs a rebirth of
Christ. Christ reincarnating himself for our intelligence
and heart in the dimensions newly discovered for experimental reality. Our Christ must be able to overspread and
illuminate these almost boundless advances."

The Abbé Breuil spent the spring of 1935 in Peking,
with a room adjoining Father Teilhard's at the house of
the Lazarist Fathers. The two friends took up their daily
routine together, working at the survey from eight in the
morning until noon and at the Peking Union Medical
College in the afternoon. It was the time of the year when
the wind blew clouds of yellow dust from the plains, but
the city was beautiful, with lilacs and apple and apricot
trees in full bloom.

Breuil walked with the aid of a cane, and his shoulders
were stooped from years of creeping along low corridors of
caves, crouching sometimes, or lying flat on his back to
study and copy the cave paintings. But in his eyes there
was the same youthful alertness as he tracked down every
clue he could to a remote past. He examined the diggings

at Chou-Kou-Tien and the specimens that had been added to the museum since his last visit to China.

One day he went with Teilhard to a wooded hill northwest of the Imperial Palace, where a large marble statue of Buddha stood beside an ancient temple. Breuil described the statue as beautiful because of the expression of the face, with its faint hint of a smile and look of joyous serenity. "I am very fond of this head, because it says something to me," Teilhard said to him. "It tells me that here is something which Christianity ought to adopt."

Dr. Frank Weidenreich, the successor to Davidson Black, arrived in April when Breuil was still in Peking. Weidenreich, a distinguished anatomist and anthropologist, had taught at the University of Frankfurt, but had left it the previous year with Hitler's rise to power. He was a visiting professor at the University of Chicago when he was offered this post by the Rockefeller Foundation. He did not take the place of Davidson Black, nor did he try, but in his quiet way, with scientific precision gained from long experience, he set about at once on the work started by Black: preparing, casting, measuring, and writing descriptions of fossil remains from Chou-Kou-Tien.

Teilhard was now free to carry out Black's second plan for an expedition to India with Helmut de Terra, but first he went to France, making the trip with Breuil on the Trans-Siberian Railway. He remained in France until the end of the summer, then boarded a ship for Bombay. "So here I am back again to my vagabond existence," he wrote to Joseph. From Bombay he went by train and by automobile to Srinagar, in northern India, where de Terra was living on a houseboat with his wife and young daughter.

From the end of September until the middle of December Teilhard and de Terra studied geological formations and searched for fossil bones and man-made tools. A young British archaeologist just out of Cambridge was with them on some of their excursions. Their headquarters were at Rawalpindi in Kashmir, and from there they explored the northwest corner of India, the Salt Range wastelands, the Sind Valley, and the Indus River delta, then down to the tropical banks of the Narbada. They crossed mountain streams that Alexander the Great had crossed when he was out to conquer the world, and they met modern pony caravans carrying rugs across the high Himalayan passes. In the Sind Valley Teilhard saw the tracks of Georges-Marie Haardt's caterpillars, still perfectly fresh, and he remembered his wait at Aksu at this same time of year and in just such a setting. "How time flies, but how vivid events remain!" Teilhard wrote to Haardt's widow, describing the scene. "This corner of Asia is full of the relics of such endeavors to conquer the world. And the expedition was one of those ventures which set their sights a little higher each time."

In the Indus delta they saw an excavation in the middle of a tamarisk jungle that partly disclosed a town that existed three thousand years ago, with red-brick dwellings, drains, streets, wells, and water system. Teilhard wrote to Breuil about his impression of the site. "We live surrounded by ideas and objects infinitely more ancient than we imagine; and yet at the same time everything is in motion. The universe is a vast thing in which we should be lost if it did not converge upon the Person."

Teilhard's search, with de Terra, was for a much older culture. They found it in neolithic tools of polished stone made ten thousand years ago, when man first planted grain and tamed the ox, and in the crudely fashioned paleolithic tools of 750,000 years ago, when man learned to make fire and to chip one stone against another to give it shape for handling. "When scrutinizing fossils or artifacts, he gave the impression that he had somehow been involved in their formation, that he could grasp their underlying significance by means of a kind of inner eye," Helmut de Terra said of Teilhard on this expedition.

There were times when they walked seven or eight hours a day. Teilhard was surprised at how young and energetic he felt. He climbed the rough hillsides or made his way through jungle paths without feeling the least bit tired. The last two weeks of the expedition were spent in central India, exploring the steep banks of the Narbada River. On the first day of their search they found bones of the same kind of animals associated with Chou-Kou-Tien: buffalo, elephant, hippopotamus, and crocodile. The next day Teilhard dug out from a layer of rock a broad-bladed, sharpened piece of quartzite, and beside it there was a hippopotamus' tooth—a silent testimony of early man's search for food, the kind he found, and the way he obtained it. The deposit proved to be a rich one, yielding stone tools of many sizes and shapes, though no fossil remains of the men who made them. Teilhard and de Terra left the government guest house where they lodged early every morning and worked along the riverbanks until late in the evening. All around them was the thick green jungle, teeming with life, for there was scarcely a living thing an Indian was allowed to kill.

Teilhard wrote his impressions of this part of the country: "Soft summer weather (21 December) ; golden light; a country shaded with mangoes and banyans, fine bushy trees like ancient oaks; tall ridges covered with thick forests (tiger jungle) ; peacocks in the jungle; crocodiles in the river; parrots in the gardens; at every corner frolicking banks of big black-faced monkeys with white ruffs; very gentle, even gracious people living in beautifully clean huts; the women red-veiled, the men in white."

He saw fakirs sitting cross-legged under mango trees, like spirits of the underworld, their half-naked bodies smeared with ashes and their long, matted hair piled up on their heads. He observed also the degrading effect of an elaborate caste system. De Terra's Indian assistant was with them on some of their excursions. He insisted on having his meals apart for, as a Brahmin, he could eat only with his equals. Father Teilhard was astounded at this custom. "No human being has the right to consider a fellow man so impure that he would not share a meal with him on religious grounds," he said. This was proof of the deadening effect of a religion obsessed by ritualism and outward form. This was as good a warning as any, he said, for a Church that had allowed itself to be dominated by rituals and forms of superstition, however disguised they were. "Sometimes I tremble in recognizing ourselves in them." Again he thought of the need for a new religion, "an improved Christianity whose personal God is no longer the 'Neolithic' landowner of times gone by, but the Soul of the world—as demanded by the cultural and religious stage we have now reached."

On his way back to China Teilhard stopped off first at Singapore, where he spent three days with the prehistorian Collings, director of the natural history museum there, then at Java for a stay of ten days. His host there was Ralph von Koenigswald, a brilliant young scientist sent out by the Dutch government to carry on the archaeological work started forty-five years earlier by Dr. Dubois. In 1931, a year after his appointment, Koenigswald discovered, in a terrace of the Solo River, fragments of eleven human skulls. They were of a later period than Java man or Peking man. The tools found at the site were of flaked and sharpened stone, of the period of Neanderthal man. Then in 1935, a few months before Teilhard's arrival,

Koenigswald found a much older deposit of crudely chipped stones. He wanted to clarify his own estimate of their age with Teilhard.

They made excursions to the south and central part of the island, stopping at villages along the way and living the life of the villagers. They slept at night in the chief's hut, and for refreshment they drank from fresh coconuts. At the sites of Koenigswald's discoveries they studied the rock strata, which Teilhard compared with those of China and India. On the floor of a cavern discovered in their exploration they found teeth of the orang, large gibbon, and bear, very much like those found in southern China. Teilhard was especially interested in the recently unearthed tools. He examined them and agreed with Koenigswald that they were of the oldest type, dating from the first warm period following the Ice Age, about 300,000 years ago. They were like the earliest ones found at Chou-Kou-Tien and the one he had found with de Terra on the banks of the Narbada. In these three widely separated places of Asia, men were beginning to use their brains, to think of a better way to obtain their food and protect themselves from the elements. These simple tools, lumps of rock chipped to a uniform shape, had once been held in a hairy fist and pounded on some object in a chopping motion, and the smaller stones, flaked to a cutting edge, had been used in the kill. What a pity it was, Teilhard said, that Davy Black was no longer there to see the result of his plans.

After an exciting four months, in settings he called the loveliest in the world, Father Teilhard boarded a Dutch steamer for Shanghai. He was eager to be back in Peking. He wondered what effect the Japanese penetration would have on conditions at the Geological Survey. But whatever had happened, he was glad he made this trip. "I come out of this new experience with the strengthened conviction that we can do nothing better in life than to take and follow the threads it offers us, step by step, towards something we do not see, but which must be there ahead, as surely as the World exists," he wrote on shipboard to a friend.

The threat of a Japanese invasion had been hanging over Peking for almost five years. In September 1931 the militarists of Japan, taking advantage of the political unrest in China, sent troops into Mukden, and within a few months they had control of all Manchuria. They established a puppet state, changed the name to Manchukuo, and installed on the throne the twenty-six-year-old Pu Yi, who, as an infant, had been the last of the Manchu emperors. Since then the Japanese had been encroaching deeper and deeper into China. When Father Teilhard arrived in Peking in February 1936, the streets were filled with Japanese soldiers in khaki uniforms and hobnailed boots, and Japanese trucks went careening past the jinrickshas.

The Chinese officials had left the city to make their headquarters in Nanking. Wong was now First Secretary under Chiang Kai-shek, Young and Bien were in southern China, Ting had died recently, and Pei was in Paris studying for his doctorate. Teilhard felt like one marooned in a wilderness, finding only four or five people in buildings that had once been so full of life. The Geological Survey of Peking was now called the North Branch, with most of its books and collections moved to Nanking.

Weidenreich was able to carry on his work at the Cenozoic Laboratory, since the Peking Union Medical College was American property and was left undisturbed for the time being. But events were happening fast that threatened the world's security. Italy had taken possession of Ethiopia in defiance of the League of Nations, Hitler had sent troops to reoccupy the demilitarized zone between Germany and France, and in Spain a civil war had broken out, with Communists and Fascists bitterly taking sides.

A more personal sorrow came to Father Teilhard that year. Soon after his return from Java he learned of the death of his mother. Six months later, in August, his sister Marguerite-Marie, Guiguite, died. "Oh Marguerite, my sister," he wrote in his grief, "as I journeyed across continents and seas, dedicated to the positive forces of the universe, passionately caught up in watching all the colors of the earth rise, you, immobile and supine, struggled with the worst shadows of the world and there, in your inmost self, metamorphosed them into light. Tell me, which of us has conducted himself best in the eyes of the Creator?"

Now only three brothers were left out of a once large and affectionate family. "I feel that a great void has opened up in my life, or rather in the world around me—a great void of which I shall become increasingly aware," Teilhard wrote to Joseph. "The only way of making life bearable again is to love and adore that which, beneath everything, animates and directs it." A favorite quotation of Father Teilhard's, which he often repeated in troubled times, was "Everything that happens is to be adored."

He plunged himself into the work to be done. There were reports to be written of his expeditions into India and Java and of a field trip south of Peking close to Shantung. The excavation at Chou-Kou-Tien still went on, though it was closely watched by the Japanese. A human jawbone of the same period as Peking man had been found at a lower level.

Koenigswald wrote of finding a very early fossil cranium of a child. Teilhard offered the young scientist advice on how to write his report, giving the details of all the conditions of the discovery, for the first public announcement. He felt a deep personal bond with Koenigswald and with de Terra. When he received an invitation from de Terra to take part in a conference on prehistory to be held in Philadelphia the following March, he requested an invitation for Koenigswald also.

Teilhard planned a trip that would take him around the world. He would be in the United States for the conference in the spring, spend the summer in France, go to Moscow for a meeting of geologists that he had been invited to attend, then on through Siberia to China. In Philadelphia he was a guest of the de Terras, and he saw again many of his colleagues. His lecture at the meeting was on the Quaternary period in China and on the evidence found that Peking man had made fire and used tools. There was a great deal of interest in the subject, and during a newspaper interview Teilhard went into more detail. To his amazement, when he read the paper the next morning he saw himself referred to in bold headlines as the "Jesuit who says that Man is descended from the apes."

Now what would his superiors have to say about that, he wondered. He had been awarded a medal for his outstanding contribution to science by a Catholic college near Philadelphia, but when he went to Boston to receive an honorary degree offered him by the Catholic University of that city, he learned that it had been withdrawn. He was told later that Rome had been alarmed over the newspaper account.

Soon after his arrival in France he went to Lyons to call on his Provincial Superior, who was also a friend. He discovered, to his surprise, that there was more tolerance and understanding, even within his Order, than he had been shown in America. No objection had been raised to his typewritten papers, now widely distributed. The editors of a conservative Catholic periodical asked him for an article on Peking man, "essentially the same things," he wrote to de Terra, "which have so much disturbed my American colleagues."

In Paris Teilhard saw a great deal of Wong, who was in Europe that summer, and of Pei, who had just finished his dissertation and was waiting to defend it for his doctorate.

An attack of recurrent fever, later diagnosed as malaria, caused a change in Father Teilhard's plans. He had to cancel his trip to Moscow, and later, after an especially severe attack, he was advised by the doctors not to go by way of Siberia on his return to China. Part of his convalescence was spent with Gabriel and his family in the old family home, Murol, on the banks of the Allier. In this soothing atmosphere, in spite of his disappointment, he felt more spiritually alive. Since he had to give up the study of the past for the time being, he felt free to look into the future. Fossil Man would be replaced by Man of Tomorrow. He outlined an essay on human energy, and ideas came to him for a book, if he could ever find time to write it, which he would simply call *Man*. "I have never known how to write anything but theses and dissertations," he said. "The highest pleasure must be to pour one's soul into a living creation: a novel, music, or better still, into another living soul."

While he was still in Auvergne a letter came from Helmut de Terra asking him to take part in an expedition, sponsored by the Carnegie Institute, to explore Southeast Asia for new clues to the origin of man. He suggested that Teilhard meet him in Burma about the middle of November. Fossil Man came out again from the background of

Father Teilhard's thoughts, and he accepted the invitation. His full strength would have returned by then.

He left for China in August, traveling by sea in a first-class cabin provided by the steamship company. China was in such a state of confusion by then that Teilhard had to go first to Japan and cross the Yellow Sea from there to reach Tientsin. The Japanese had possession of all northern China, had landed troops in Shanghai, and were sending bombs down on Nanking and Canton. The future of the Cenozoic Laboratory, as well as the Geological Survey, was uncertain. There was a possibility also that Chou-Kou-Tien would fall into other hands. Teilhard hesitated to leave Peking at a time like this. "And it would have been so important for me to go to Burma," he wrote in early November. "I shall wait a little longer before I finally decide, but I am very much afraid that it will be impossible to be in two minds about where my duty lies: I must stay here."

During that month he moved from his pleasant quarters with the Lazarist Fathers to Chabanel Hall, a Jesuit House that had recently been established for young recruits, mostly Spanish and Canadian, to learn Chinese. The place had many drawbacks. It was in an out-of-the-way area, so far from the city Teilhard had to spend an hour and a half of his day going to and from the laboratory and office. The buildings were like barracks, stripped to the barest essentials, and the priests were under the same strict discipline as the students, with everyone in his room by eight at night. Teilhard took advantage of this leisure to make a start on his book *Man,* though the superior of the house had heard enough about his ideas to regard him with suspicion.

November passed, and Teilhard was resigned to calling

off the expedition in Burma, when young Pei arrived in Peking. He offered to take on the work at the Geological Survey in his place, which left Teilhard free to carry out his plans.

Helmut de Terra and his wife, Rhoda, with Dr. Movius, a prehistorian from Harvard, and his wife, had been in Burma a month when Teilhard left Peking. He was delayed even further by having to change ships three times along the way. From Rangoon, following instructions de Terra had left for him, he took a paddle steamer up the Irrawaddy River to a landing place near Mandalay, where the field work had been started.

The group of five spent the next three months exploring the upper Irrawaddy valley and the High Shan plateau, close to the Chinese border. They drove through tropical forests of bamboo and teakwood, home of the rhinoceros, tiger, buffalo, crocodile, and small deer, animals of the same species that had inhabited northern China and the Himalayas long before the appearance of man. And from the dense branches of the trees could be heard the chattering sound of gibbons. As in India, Teilhard felt a fresh energy and a renewal of his youth. He was able to keep up with the younger men, walking all day without feeling tired. They examined the high riverbanks, very like the banks of the Narbada, and searched in limestone caves and in a ruby mine.

The expedition was the success they had hoped for. They studied the geological features of the region and discovered a connection with other parts of Asia from India to Java. They collected hundreds of rough, primitive tools of the same type and age as those found with Java man and Peking man, and they unearthed fossil remains of animals of the same kind as had been found in southern China and Yunnan.

In the ancient city of Pagan, now little more than a bazaar, the group was lodged in a luxurious guest house the government had built for George V when he was Prince of Wales. It was set in a garden of roses, poinsettias, and hibiscus in full bloom. Gaily colored parakeets flitted among the bamboo clumps. From the veranda Father Teilhard looked out on the Irrawaddy under a cloudless sky, catching the reflection of the low, green hills on the opposite bank. He was reminded of the Nile in Egypt, and he felt again the fascination for the East.

From Burma the expedition moved on to Java to examine the human fossils Koenigswald and his associate had discovered over the past six years. In addition to the child's cranium Koenigswald had found in 1936, a second Pithecanthropus, or Ape Man, skull had been found six months before. This was of an adult and resembled the one found by Dr. Dubois. Koenigswald led the expedition through the central and eastern part of the island to the sites where many of the fossils had been found. They made their way through swamps and jungle paths and spent one hot, humid day gathering stone tools by the Solo River. The men compared notes on the limestone and volcanic formations and discussed the question of whether these prehistoric beings, Java man, Peking man, and Neanderthal man, were offshoots of the branch from which modern man was descended. They had evolved enough above the animal to make fire and use tools, but they had dropped out along the way and become extinct.

Teilhard left Java before the end of the expedition, for he had been uneasy about what was happening in Peking. He found conditions the same as when he had left in December, day by day living in an atmosphere of uncertainty and uneasiness. The city had become an odd mixture of Tokyo and Peking, with as many geisha girls as elegant Chinese women. Work at the Chou-Kou-Tien site had to be stopped, caught as it was in a no-man's-land between Japanese troops on the plains and Chinese Reds in the mountains. With Pei to assist him, however, Teilhard was able to keep on with his normal routine of work in spite of the reduced staff. "I find it difficult not to smile when I see myself so absorbed in describing a fossil bone," he said. He published several scientific articles and wrote a report of the Burma expedition. And in the evenings he went on with his book on Man, beginning with Matter, which holds the germ from which all life has evolved, including Man.

His friends in Paris had persuaded him, a few months earlier, to submit his name for an appointment in the Sorbonne's Paleontological Laboratory. Soon after his return from Burma he received word that his nomination had been accepted and that his superiors in Rome had given their consent to his return to France. This did not mean he would abandon his work in the East. "I am still needed in China, and I feel I need it still more," he said. But it did mean a longer stay in his native country and an acceptance, at last, of his ideas. "I can hardly believe it is true," he said when the time drew near for his departure.

Father Licent was recalled to France that summer because of his health and the unsettled conditions of the East, and Pierre Leroy took his place as director of the museum at Tientsin. When Teilhard left China to travel by way of America, Leroy went with him as far as Japan. There they both tried to see what could be done to allow the scientific work in Tientsin and Peking to be carried on without interference.

Teilhard's circle of American friends had grown so that he allowed himself several weeks in California, Boston, and New York. It was not until the first week of November that he was in Paris and settled down to his work at the Paleontological Laboratory. He had an office next to Breuil's, and Boule still came down to the museum twice a week. Boule had grown old, but his mind was still alert, and he liked to talk about the Golden Age of Prehistory. In a way it was as if time had stood still and it was 1920 again, but for Father Teilhard there was a great difference. He was so sought after that he scarcely had any time to himself. They came, he said, from various and unexpected corners of society, searching and asking about a broad and idealistic representation of life. In talking with them he felt a greater understanding of his own thoughts. He wanted to see a new type of research develop. "It is still egotistic, meaningless," he said. "Scientists have a narrow soul, a short sight, and generally an underdeveloped heart. They are dry and inhuman and so often ugly. All this because they are burrowing without looking at the sky. I dream to open this sky, right in the line of their tunnels."

Soon after his arrival in France he was summoned to Lyons for a talk with his Provincial Superior. It was a repetition of the old story. One of his unpublished papers had come into the hands of the General Superior of his Order in Rome. It was not a bad one, Teilhard remarked, but not the type he would have selected for Roman criticism. To make matters worse, the superior of Chabanel Hall had complained to Rome that he was disturbing the minds of the young Jesuit scholastics there. Teilhard was resigned to the new restrictions placed on him, but now there was a question of whether he would be allowed to return to Peking.

"At bottom they do not dislike me," he explained to one who thought he should break with his Order. "They are only bewildered and anxious to defend tradition. Since I don't want (and since it would be a mistake) to break off, I have logically to adjust myself somewhat more." He was again in that paradoxical position he had been in for years, with his colleagues in France supporting him and Rome holding him under suspicion. But one of the Jesuit fathers from Tientsin who visited Rome that winter talked on his behalf, and everything was settled for a while.

The following spring the superior from Lyons came to Paris in a disturbed mood. Another of Teilhard's papers, this one stronger than the earlier one, had been sent to Rome. The superior was a fair man, and friendly toward Father Teilhard, though he did not entirely understand him, and he left in better spirits after listening to explanations and arguments from Teilhard's Jesuit colleagues. It was finally agreed that Teilhard would be allowed to go back to China, and return again to France, following the same back-and-forth pattern.

When he left in June Teilhard chose again to travel by way of America. It was strange the way America and France were interlocking in his life, he said. There were times when he found himself wondering where he did belong. He spent the month of July in the United States, with that feeling of rejuvenation the country always gave him. But however tempting it was to stay, he knew he must move on. "I feel in an unmistakable way that if I do not make the next step to China, I shall not know where to put my foot next. There are links in my life."

He reached Kobe, Japan, in time to hear the news that Nazi Germany and Soviet Russia had signed a ten-year non-aggression treaty. Teilhard sailed to China on a small, overcrowded Japanese steamer. He found Tientsin flooded, with water in the streets so high he could have reached the Jesuit house only by boat, so he went directly to Peking. Three days after his arrival, on September 3rd, France and Germany were at war.

IX
Again,
a World at War

"AND NOW WHAT! Such terrible news all over the world, with so many clouds left to burst. (Russia? Italy?)" There had been tension throughout Europe when Father Teilhard left France. People spoke of it as the Cold War, the Phony War, the War of Nerves, and none but the political leaders wanted to see it go beyond that. The enthusiasm and fighting spirit of the First World War were missing. "Would it be possible that we are gradually getting vaccinated against mere brutal violence?" Teilhard asked.

In China the systematic invasion by the Japanese had been going on for two years, and there had been guerrilla warfare in the north and the south for longer than that. Peking, however, was relatively quiet, unchanged except for the presence of the Japanese. There were the same curved roofs under a blue sky, the same street cries of the

vendors, the same yellow dust blown in by the wind. In the
foreign colony the friendships among the different nationalities were unaffected for the time being. From this
distance the war seemed unreal, like a dream not understood. The newspapers and radios were so filled with
propaganda on one side or the other that it was impossible
to know just what was going on. And the mail was slow in
coming through.

"Where are you, and what can you do? Help me to feel
what is happening and bring it into my life," Teilhard
wrote to his cousin Marguerite. He wrote to Breuil, to the
Bégouëns, and to Gabriel and Joseph, wanting to know
how they were affected by the war. Had his brothers been
called up? And what about Joseph's son Olivier? He was
twenty now and eligible to serve. "What a humiliating
position mine is, while your life—all your lives—is completely altered and engulfed in the immediacy of the
conflict." Should he go back to France? he asked. At fifty-
nine he could not take an active part as in 1914, but, he
said, there surely must be something he could do.

As the weeks passed, he found this complete lack of
news hard to bear. Finally in November letters from
France began coming in, but they were two months old
and much could have happened in the meantime. Gabriel
had been mobilized in the balloon service near Tours.
Joseph had not been called, but his son was expecting to
be soon. "I have no choice but to watch and wait," Teilhard said.

There was enough material in the drawers of the
laboratories to keep him busy cataloguing and describing
for two years, even with Chou-Kou-Tien closed. Weidenreich was on a year's leave in New York, but Pei was still
working with him. Teilhard wanted to make a field trip to

Yunnan for more information on that southwest part of China adjoining Burma, but he was advised against it.

One Sunday in early spring he went on a picnic with some American friends to one of the temples still accessible in the Western Hills on the outskirts of Peking. They roasted mutton Mongol style by holding the pieces with long chopsticks over the fire. Teilhard brought along his geological hammer and went exploring. This was the first time he had felt a contact with the earth since the Burma expedition two years before. He remembered field trips he had taken in the past, from the first ones with Father Licent under the most primitive conditions. Now he looked back to this time as the good old days. Poor Father Licent, confined to a small room in a Jesuit House in Paris, his only collection a cardboard box of insects, must also have looked back nostalgically to the times when he roamed over the hills and deserts and wild riverbanks of north China.

Tientsin suffered more than Peking from the Japanese invasion. The Jesuit School for Higher Studies, like all the other European and American buildings, was barricaded by barbed wire put up by the Japanese and guarded by arrogant sentries. During the flood of the past autumn, water had stood two feet deep in the museum galleries, damaging several of the specimens. The rector of the school suggested to Leroy that he move the collection to Peking. The French Embassy offered a place for the museum and laboratory in the embassy guard barracks, and Teilhard agreed to help in the tremendous task of dismantling, sorting, and packing the thousands of embalmed and fossil specimens, from beetles to elephant bones. After the move the name of the museum was changed to the Institute of Geobiology, and its purpose was broadened to study geological and biological evolution throughout Asia.

Chabanel Hall was too far from the French Embassy to
make it practical for Father Teilhard to live there any
longer. In early June he moved to a house provided for
him, Leroy, another Jesuit, and a member of the French
legation. After Chabanel Hall, with its rigid discipline and
unfriendly atmosphere, this was a warm and pleasant
place, the nearest to a home Teilhard had had during his
eighteen years in China. He brought his books, his paintings, a favorite chair, and the best of his collections. A cook
looked after the household, and in the private courtyard
there were fruit trees, chickens, a dog, and two kittens.

The four friends had just settled down in their new
quarters when, on June 14th, the incredible news came
over the radio that the French government had collapsed
under a German invasion. A new government was formed
and an armistice was signed agreeing to Hitler's terms.
The northern part of France and all the Atlantic seaboard
would remain under German Occupation. The French in
Peking were deeply shocked over this defeat. It was
strange, Teilhard said, to feel he had only half a country—
strange, too, to hear German and Italian propaganda coming out of Paris. Again he felt a sense of helplessness. What
would be left in the long run? Could they escape revolu-
tion? He asked questions and tried to find the answers.
Whatever happened, there was still the earth. Once he had
been so sure that something good was growing, something
that could have been a ferment for the world. Perhaps the
seed was still there, ready to develop on a rejuvenated
ground. Perhaps the world was paying now for something
fine to come.

His book on Man, now called, after an earlier essay,
The Phenomenon of Man, was finished. "My best and only
way to fight for a better world," he said of it. He had three

copies typed, but before it could be considered for publication, it would have to pass the censors of his Order. An
American friend in the diplomatic service in Peking
offered to take one of the copies to Washington and send it
from there by way of the American Embassy in Paris.

The first letters since the fall of Paris came through in
September. Teilhard learned that his two brothers and
their families were safe in Auvergne, part of the unoccu-
pied zone. The Teillard de Chambon cousins were also in
their old home. But where were Breuil, the Bégouëns,
Boule? Father d'Ouince, a good friend who had often
come to Teilhard's defense when there was trouble with
the authorities at Rome, was now a political prisoner in
Paris. How many others suffered the same fate?

It was impossible for Teilhard to return to France
then. "I still hope for a spark under these ashes," he said,
but he didn't feel inclined to try to force his way back to a
France under German rule. He turned his thoughts to
America, "my second fatherland," he called it. There was
something deep and strong and free there.

In his letter to the General Superior of his Order telling about his book *The Phenomenon of Man,* he also
asked permission to take part in a conference in New York
in September 1941. It would be a meeting of scientists,
philosophers, and theologians on the subject of the relation between science and religion. The answer came three
months later, in March 1941. His participation in the
conference was not approved; however, he might send in a
written communication, subject to the censors' approval,
of course. The authorities also consented to look over the
manuscript of his book for a sympathetic revision.

Teilhard had already worked on his lecture, and the
paper was ready to be sent immediately. His theme was the
same one he had been repeating for so long, of Life's slow,

steady movement forward, from the protozoa to Man, then emerging into Thought. Even here it did not come to a stop. It is still advancing along its path, surmounting, as now, periods of afflictions, upheavals, and war. "The ship that bears us is still making headway." But the movement is slow and imperceptible. The human group is still young, with millions of years ahead of it in which to develop. Countless human beings, forces, and ideas are yet to be born, or discovered, or applied and synthesized.

The paper was written in answer to the wave of pessimism that was sweeping the world. "Whether from immobilist reaction, sick pessimism, or simply pose, it has become good form to deride or mistrust anything that looks like faith in the future," Teilhard remarked. "I wish to show in this paper that, however bitter our disillusionment with human goodness in recent years, there are stronger scientific reasons than ever before for believing that we do really progress and that we can advance much further still, provided that we are clear about the direction in which progress lies, and are resolved to take the right road."

War clouds began gathering over the Pacific, and a clash between Japan and the United States seemed inevitable. The Americans were gradually being recalled from China, and the Japanese in occupation were becoming more firmly entrenched. The Peking Union Medical College was faced with the problem of what to do about the findings from Chou-Kou-Tien. The buildings were technically American property and safe, so far, from being taken over by the Japanese, but it was not certain how long this would last. Father Teilhard had gone to inspect the site at Chou-Kou-Tien, under a guard of watchful Japanese, soon after his return from France, and found that the place had been thoroughly rifled. Though the valuable part of the collection was in Peking, this was an indication of what would happen if the Japanese could get their hands on it.

There was a discussion about what could be done. It was too great a risk to send the collection to a quieter part of the country, or to keep it in some secret hiding place in Peking. Finally Wong, with the permission of Chiang Kai-shek, made an arrangement with the American Embassy to have the collection taken to the United States for safe keeping until the danger was past. On December 5th a special train pulled out of the Peking station with a contingent of American Marines being evacuated and carefully packed boxes containing a cargo that has been compared in value to the crown jewels of a nation. The train headed toward Chingwangtao, a seacoast town a short distance away, where the American ship *President Harrison* was waiting at the harbor.

Two days later the Japanese, without warning, dropped bombs on Pearl Harbor, thus bringing the war around the entire world. In the turmoil that followed, the cargo of fossils disappeared and no trace of it has ever been found. Peking man, unknown and hidden in the earth for half a million years, had gone back into oblivion. Thanks to the patient and exacting work of Black and Weidenreich, copies of the pieces are in museums in New York, London, and Uppsala.

Japanese troops swept through all of Southeast Asia, taking over one country after another. In Java Koenigswald was put in one concentration camp and his wife and child in another. He had had the foresight to distribute the original fossils found there among friends he could trust, substituting copies for display in the museum. Since France, under German domination, was no longer in the war, the French in Asia were spared the indignities suffered by other nationals, but certain restrictions were imposed, and red armbands were issued identifying them as enemy aliens.

Father Teilhard had been barred from field work for two years, and now, since the Japanese authorities had taken over all Chinese and American institutions, the Geological Survey and the Cenozoic Laboratory were closed to him. He and Leroy continued with their Institute of Geobiology, but they had to accept a Japanese paleontologist as an associate.

"As far as the external life is concerned, almost nothing is changed for me, too little, in fact," Teilhard assured a friend in a letter. He followed his normal routine, beginning with Mass at seven in the morning. At eight he was in his office, where Leroy joined him for a half-hour chat, then he spent the rest of the morning writing and thinking. He gathered all the scraps of paper on which, at odd moments, he had jotted down ideas that came to him on philosophy, science, or religion and copied the ones he thought worth keeping in a notebook. In the afternoon he worked in the Geobiological laboratory, or on scientific articles, which were published by the institute. At five, when the work of the day was over, Teilhard and Leroy went calling on friends. "It was in these gatherings you saw the real Father Teilhard," Leroy said. "His very presence brought an atmosphere of assurance and confidence."

Teilhard's American friends had all gone except Grabau, who had grown old and sick and kept himself secluded in his home. Of his Chinese friends, all but Pei had gone to southern China. On the other hand, the French diplomatic staff was now concentrated in Peking. They formed a close, intimate group, as their quarters were located some distance from the heart of the city and their movements were restricted by the Japanese. They continued the Sunday picnics, started by the Americans, in

the Western Hills. Always, as soon as they arrived, Teilhard, wearing khaki trousers and a felt hat, went off with
his geological hammer to explore the ridges until time for
lunch. As there was no other place accessible to him, he
made a detailed study of these hills, collecting specimens of
rock, with an occasional fossil plant embedded in them.
The result was an article that he called "The Genesis of
the Western Hills."

At times Teilhard was able to send a message to relatives or friends in France, but there was always a long wait
for a reply to reach him. His brother Gabriel died in 1941,
but a year passed before he could receive the message.
Marcellin Boule was dead, and so was Mlle. Zanta.

In 1943 Abbé Breuil sent him an air-mail letter, limited to twenty-five words, through the Red Cross: "Long
stay here. Health, work, first rate. Your news six weeks old.
Request more."

The message was sent from South Africa. Three years
before the discovery of Peking man, the skull of a strange
being had been unearthed in the region around Johannesburg. It was of a child with a cranial capacity no larger
than that of present-day apes, but his teeth were human
and the set of the skull showed that he had walked upright.
Here was a distinct species, a connecting link between ape
and man, and he was classified as Australopithecus, meaning Southern Ape. By 1938 two adult skulls had been
found that gave a better picture of this creature, higher
than an animal, yet not quite human. The war brought a
halt to excavations in Africa as in other parts of the world,
so Breuil could only study, measure, and write descriptions
of the material already collected. Teilhard's reply to
Breuil was: "Envy you. Well in mind and body. Publishing much, but old."

His life of close confinement was against everything in

his nature, and there were periods of depression that took all his strength of will to conquer. His despair, however, was of the immediate present, for never once did he lose faith in the future, that distant goal toward which Man has been reaching since his beginning. Even this war, with the unleashing of hatred spreading out as wide as the earth itself, was serving to bind mankind together, he believed. "A thick fog of confusion and dissension is at present drifting over the world. Indeed one might say that men have never before more vehemently rebuffed and detested one another than they do now, when everything drives them closer together."

Whole armies were being moved from one hemisphere to another, thousands of refugees were scattered like seeds in the wind, all over the world. Modern airports were being built on islands once remote and almost inaccessible. Underdeveloped regions were being drawn into the industrialized world. "Brutal and harsh though the circumstances have been, who can fail to perceive the inevitable consequences of this new stirring of the human dough?"

The war ended in Europe on May 8, 1945, with the unconditional surrender of Germany. It was a relief, Teilhard said, but not a joy. "At least here and now, this brutal victory of Man over Man is not victory on the part of humanity." Three months later the United States dropped the atom bomb, a new and terrifying weapon, on Hiroshima, followed by another on Nagasaki. Japan surrendered on August 14th, bringing an end to the war after six weary years of fighting. The Japanese withdrew from China, and then the Americans arrived. "The town is rejuvenated," Teilhard wrote. "Everybody likes them; they are so full of vitality, so generous." The red armbands that were the mark of enemy aliens could now be discarded.

Father Teilhard received an official invitation from his Provincial Superior at Lyons, asking him to return to France without delay. The British consulate issued him a visa, and an American general had him flown in an army plane to Shanghai, where he boarded a ship for England. On May 3rd, two days after his sixty-fifth birthday, he was back in Paris.

Joseph had his offices there, and the two brothers were reunited after the long separation. Breuil was also in Paris, but for a visit only, and was planning to go back to Africa, where excavations had begun. Teilhard had a longing to be back in the field again and began making plans to join Breuil in Johannesburg some time the following year, 1947. He wanted de Terra as part of the expedition, and he wrote to Barbour saying, "If only you could come along!"

In the meantime he was spending the busiest and most exciting months of his life. When he was last in Paris he had been surprised to see how large his following had grown. Now he was overwhelmed. It was something like a rising tide, he said. There were so many visitors, telephone calls, letters to be answered, and requests for lectures and articles that there were not enough hours in the day for him. "Like the Buddha, I should like to have ten pairs of hands, ten heads, or only a good and efficient secretary," he remarked. Young and old came to him, eagerly seeking for a readjustment of the world and of their own thoughts. Was this the fermentation he had hoped for? he wondered.

He went to Lyons that summer for a meeting with his Provincial Superior, and in August he was back in his native Auvergne with Joseph and his family at their big, old-fashioned country home, Les Moulins. Looking out on the peaceful landscape of meadows and woods, with the chain of volcanic hills on the horizon, he realized how much he was still deeply rooted spiritually to this place. For six quiet weeks he worked on the manuscript of *The Phenomenon of Man*. He had been given hope that, after a few changes, it would pass the censors at Rome.

Since his return to France five of his essays had been published, including one on the psychological effects of the atom bomb. In these essays, and in the many lectures he gave the following winter, there ran the same message, of Man as a phenomenon, still in the process of evolution, still rising above himself. Something of the same old story, he said of it, but he was continually rewording it so its meaning would be clear.

Everything was going smoothly for his trip to Africa in 1947. There was no objection from the superiors of his Order. He would be sponsored by Weidenreich, now with the American Museum of Natural History, and by Dr. Fejos of the Wenner-Gren Foundation in New York, and he would be accepted as an independent member of the University of California expedition. George Barbour made plans to meet him in Johannesburg, and Breuil was already there waiting for him.

Teilhard planned to leave France the middle of July, but on the first of June he was suddenly stricken with a heart attack. For two weeks he hovered between life and death, then a long convalescence followed. "I have to call on all the philosophy of my faith to make part of myself and put to constructive use what is, in itself, heartbreaking," he wrote to Breuil. The African trip seemed so exactly the next step for him to take. Now the doctors could give him no assurance that he could ever take up field work again. "In any case," he said, "I have decided to take this blow as a touch of the spur rather than a check of the bridle," he added. If an active life was no longer possible, he would turn from Fossil Man to Living Man.

By the end of July he was able to leave the clinic for a convalescent home, where he was cared for by the Sisters of Mercy. While there he was made an officer of the Legion of Honor for outstanding services to the intellectual and scientific influence of France. But there also came, in September, a letter from the Superior General of his Order forbidding him to publish for the time being anything in the line of philosophy or theology. Father Teilhard tried to find comfort in his favorite quotation, "Everything that happens is to be adored," but now he added, "Provided that we allow God to give a meaning to events, even seemingly absurd, through our confidence and faith." As his strength returned, he was able to give a few lectures and do a little writing between periods of rest. That, he said, was quite fair play and recognized as such by his Superior General.

Soon after he had left the convalescent home Teilhard received an invitation from the American scientist George Gaylord Simpson to work with him at the American Museum of Natural History. Nothing, he felt, could do more to rejuvenate him in heart and mind than to be back in America, working with old friends again. Granger was dead, but both Weidenreich and Koenigswald were members of the staff.

By the time he received permission from Rome for the trip, Teilhard was ready, with passport and visa, and at the end of February he was on his way to New York. He was given a room at the Jesuit headquarters, the St. Ignatius Residence on Park Avenue, and the Wenner-Gren Foundation offered him an office on the top floor of their building. Both places were within walking distance, through Central Park, to the Museum of Natural History, where he spent some time every day. He was still limited in his activities and this was his first time in America without making field trips, but he managed to see many of his old friends. George Barbour and his wife called on him, and he visited Dr. Movius and his wife, his companions on the Burma trip, in Boston.

The three months in America were like a tonic to Teilhard, and when he left in May he was ready to go back to his busy life in Paris. Dr. Fejos asked him to return to New York the following year and give a series of lectures at the Wenner-Gren Foundation. And, when he had been in Paris a few days, the College of France asked him to become a candidate for a professorship, taking the place of the Abbé Breuil, who would soon retire. Teilhard submitted both of these requests to Rome, asking for permission to accept them.

Three months later a cordial letter came from the Father General himself, inviting Teilhard to Rome in October for a discussion of these matters. The letter was so friendly in tone that Teilhard had reason to hope that he would be permitted to publish *The Phenomenon of Man*. The revised version had been approved by his Provincial Superior at Lyons and sent on to Rome over a year ago. There was a possibility that *The Divine Milieu* would be approved also. "If that goes as I hope," Teilhard wrote to George Barbour, "there is a strong chance that I shall receive authorization to present myself to the College of France, and eventually to give six lectures in America."

In this frame of mind he left for Rome in the beginning of October and spent a full month there. During this time he had only one talk with the Father General, but he was pleased with the interview. "I don't think we see the world the same way," Teilhard said, "but he is extremely open-minded, frank, and he wants one to speak frankly to him." Teilhard explained, in a friendly but honest way, his point of view, and he also gave his opinion of the weakness and the strength of Christianity.

Though this was his first time in Rome, he took none of the usual sightseeing trips of the tourist. Except for a late afternoon stroll, he seldom left the Jesuit headquarters. He was given the manuscript of *The Phenomenon of Man* with ten long pages of criticism, and he spent his mornings revising and trying once more to satisfy the authorities without distorting his meaning. He described it as little more than dotting the i's and crossing the t's, but when it was finished, with an epilogue added to it, he felt it was an improvement over the original draft.

On Teilhard's last day in Rome, a representative of the Father General advised him against accepting the offer of the College of France. The other matters, he was told, were still left open. Three months later he received word from Rome that he would not be given permission to lecture in the United States and that *The Divine Milieu* was not approved for publication. *The Phenomenon of Man* was still not decided upon.

"In our souls, as on the sea, storms subside gradually," Teilhard wrote that winter to a troubled friend. "Hold your course toward confidence, not exactly in the World, but in the Heart of the World, that is, in the center of convergence toward which I am convinced that we fall, by an attraction more irresistible and just as universal as that imposed on the heavenly bodies by the Einsteinian curve. That is all I live by, myself, these days."

There were some who attacked Teilhard's beliefs, through public speeches and pamphlets, and others who came to his defense. "Has he not already done magnificent work in correcting the theory of evolution from within," one said, "in snatching the weapon from the hand of the materialist and turning it against him and so offering the theologian a theory of the universe both evolutionary and uncompromisingly spiritual?"

Teilhard received his country's highest honor when he was elected to the French Academy of Sciences. "What with the decoration, I am getting to be a regular grand old man. What would dear old Boule say if he were here—what scorn!" he remarked. He accepted the honor as having been offered him more for his ideas than for his science. Perhaps, he said, Rome would think twice before banning him. And then, on the other hand, they may think more than twice before letting him publish.

The following month he received his answer. It was a definite "No" to the publication of *The Phenomenon of Man,* and he was again reminded that he should confine his writings and lectures to pure science. When friends asked once more the question he had been asked so many times, why he remained with the Order when by leaving it he could be free, his answer was that by doing this he would be breaking the thread that bound him to the will of God. "I am not to be pitied as a persecuted man," he insisted. He had been shown such consideration and even affection at Rome that he was sure this decision was meant for his own protection. At the same time he felt that he had become the subject of too much controversy, with his speeches and articles quoted in public print so often that it could be embarrassing to Rome. It would be best for him to leave France for a while, he decided. Once he would have gone quietly back to China, but that way was closed to him now. This time it would be America, but first he would make that long-planned trip to South Africa.

X
Africa and America

THERE HAD NEVER BEEN any objection from Rome to any
of Father Teilhard's scientific writings or lectures, and
when it was necessary, as now, for him to leave France, he
was always allowed to choose whichever place he felt was
best suited to his research and studies. He was given permission to make the African trip and to go from there to
the United States. The Wenner-Gren Foundation again
offered to sponsor him, and George Barbour agreed a
second time to meet him in Africa. Only Breuil, who had
come back to France, would be missing.

Teilhard sailed from England and arrived at Capetown
at the end of July, the winter season in South Africa. From
there he went by train to Johannesburg, where Barbour
was waiting for him. With their South African colleagues
they examined the collections in the laboratories and

visited excavation sites. Again Teilhard and Barbour made geological observations and compared notes, as they had done in China. Memories of China came often to Father Teilhard while he was in Africa. He saw fruit trees as red as in March on the Western Hills. The air felt like that of a Peking spring, but without the sandy winds. A cloudless sky was like the unchanging Peking sky.

He had not recovered his full strength, and as his periods of activity had to be followed by periods of rest, his companions made this easy for him. Since 1947, the time of his first planned visit, many more individual Australopithecine remains had been found, twenty-five in one fissure alone, so that more was known of what this being was like and the kind of life he must have led. Though he walked upright, it was with the side to side swing of an ape. Unlike the other apes, he had become a meat eater, though there was no evidence found of his use of tools or fire. "How on earth did such creatures manage to live and defend themselves!" Teilhard exclaimed as he examined a small, human-like canine. Without fangs or claws, the weapons of other animals, and without the intelligence of man, he must have developed a certain amount of cunning and skill to have survived and dominated his surroundings as he did. But he had failed to cross the boundary separating animal from man, and had died out as a species. He was hominid, Teilhard wrote in a report of his trip. "Hominid all the same does not mean human."

Of all the human fossil remains found over the past century, beginning with the skull dug out of a limestone cave in Neander Valley, not one had the shape of Piltdown man. Neanderthal man, Java man, Peking man, Broken Hill man, found recently near Rhodesia, and now this preman, Australopithecus, all had an ape-like cranium and man-like jaws. Only Piltdown had the brain capacity of modern man with the muzzle-like jaw of an ape.

Through the stone tools that had been found in South Africa, Teilhard could follow man in all his early stages of evolution. He examined the roughly chipped pebbles and called them the earliest evidence of human industry re-corded anywhere in the world. He found an amazing continuity leading from these first crude tools of about 500,000 years ago on to the perfectly symmetrical stone hand-axes made 400,000 years later. In a lecture he gave to the South African Geological Society Teilhard confessed that once he had believed that man originated in Europe. Then, with the discovery of Java man and Peking man, he had looked upon Asia as man's birthplace. Now, since coming to Africa, he realized that man was decidedly older and deeper-rooted here. In Europe and Asia man was rela-tively a newcomer. He pictured the migration of man's earliest ancestors, starting out from this continent and spreading like a wave over the whole earth.

This renewed contact with the past led Teilhard's thoughts, as always, to the future. Knowledge of the past, he said, was empty if it did not follow that irresistible human movement that is still going on in and around us. He spoke of evolution as the hand of God drawing us to ourselves.

On October 12th, while he was waiting at Capetown for his ship to sail, he wrote a letter to the Father General, expressing his loyalty and at the same time explaining exactly where he stood. "I do this without forgetting that you are the 'General,' but at the same time (as during our too-short interview three years ago) with the frankness that is one of the Society's most precious assets." He re-peated his compelling belief in the convergence of all things toward Christ. "What might have been taken for obstinacy or disrespect in my attitude for the last thirty years is simply the result of my absolute inability to contain my own feeling of wonderment." He could no more change this feeling than he could change his age or the color of his eyes. Having said this, he went on to express his loyalty to the Church and to his Order. Never, he said, had Christ seemed more real to him, more personal, more immense. "How, then, can I believe there is any evil in the road I am following?" He realized that Rome had its reasons for the attitude taken toward him, and he wanted to assure the Father General that, in spite of any apparent evidence to the contrary, he was resolved to remain a "child of obedience."

There was no separation in his mind of his religious from his scientific beliefs, yet when he was told of a series of lectures in Scotland where he might present the basic ideas of *The Phenomenon of Man,* his answer was that he would be unfaithful to his vows and would be violating part of himself even to consider it.

In summing up his African trip Teilhard wrote: "All this has finally strengthened my passionate conviction, as I look at and beyond the Austropithecines and the foundation of the continents, that man is in some obscure way discovering (or seeing as it manifests itself), a new face of God: the evolutive God of cosmogenesis."

Teilhard sailed to New York by way of South America. For the past three years an Austrian who had immigrated to Argentina had been doing some interesting research in the prehistory of this part of the world. Teilhard spent a week in Buenos Aires, where he examined the collections in the museum and again compared and contrasted the geology of two continents. He saw land formations and sandstone of the same kind as was to be found in Africa.

Traces of man in America went back no more than ten thousand years. Here he saw the terminus, right to the end of the journey, of a movement of human expansion that started in the region of Africa he had just left. It had been a long, slow journey of several hundred thousand years, through Europe, crossing the whole breadth of Asia, and the length of North America.

After his arrival in New York Father Teilhard received a message from the new Provincial Superior at Lyons, warning him that the situation in Rome had become somewhat strained as far as he was concerned. This meant that his stay in America, planned as a temporary one, was to be extended indefinitely. "It will be 1925 all over again, with New York instead of China. The only thing is, I am now seventy," Teilhard said. And to a friend in France he wrote, "I can't help feeling rather depressed at being cut off from Paris. However, there are compensations. I'll get over it, and the important thing is that I can do some good here."

His many friends in America made his exile easier, and since the United States was beginning to take a lead in scientific research, scientists from over the world were attracted here. Teilhard often had reunions with old friends from France and from his Peking days. He was asked by Dr. Fejos to become an associate director of the Wenner-Gren Foundation, and through this he became absorbed in work more fascinating than any he had ever known. His interest had now turned from Asia to prehistory in Africa, and the foundation also was beginning to direct its attention to some of the projects there.

In July 1953, Teilhard, as representative of the foundation, was sent on his second trip to Africa to help organize research in all the region south of the Sahara. He visited three centers of excavation and saw what great progress had been made even in the two years since his first visit. A human skull had been found at Hopefield, east of Saldanha Bay, near Capetown. Fossil bones of animals and stone tools giving a clue to its age were taken from the same site. The skull was of a Neanderthal type, thick and flattened, with ridges over the eyes and a bulge in the back, like all the other skulls of early man with the one exception of Piltdown man.

In November, after Teilhard's return to New York, a startling paper was published by three British scientists that solved the mystery of Piltdown man once and for all. It was a hoax. The skull was human, of a period no earlier than about ten thousand years, but the jaw was that of a modern orangutan, dyed with iron oxide to look ancient, and with teeth filed to the pattern of human teeth. Kenneth Oakley of the British Museum had used a recently developed chemical test of dating by measuring the amount of fluorine in the fossil bones and comparing them with other specimens from the same deposit.

Teilhard wrote a letter of congratulations to Oakley. Anatomically speaking, he said, Piltdown man had been a kind of monster, and from a paleontological point of view it was equally shocking that a "dawn man" could have been found in England. "Therefore I am fundamentally pleased by your conclusions, in spite of the fact that, sentimentally speaking, it spoilt one of my brightest and earliest paleontological memories," he added.

It had been forty years since Teilhard found the fragment of an elephant's molar that had so excited Smith-Woodward, and a year after that, on a short visit to England while he was working under Boule, he had found a human canine. He could look back on his association with Dawson and Smith-Woodward as the beginning of his interest in the origin of man and in the phenomenon of man's continuing evolution.

With the solution of one mystery, there was another to take its place. Who was responsible for the hoax? Neither Dawson nor Woodward was alive to defend himself. Teilhard refused to believe either was guilty, and he looked for explanations. The Piltdown pit was a dumping place for the farms and cottages, and in winter, when it was flooded, the water from the clay could quickly stain anything thrown in it. He had seen a freshly sawed bone from a butcher shop stained almost as deep a brown as the ape's jaw Dawson had found. "Had a collector possessing some ape bones thrown his discarded specimens into the pit?" he wrote. "The idea sounds fantastic but, in my opinion, no more fantastic than to make Dawson the perpetrator of a hoax."

Whoever the guilty person was, he obviously had a knowledge of paleontology. Stone tools and fossil remains of animals associated with early man had been planted in the same deposits. Some of the fossils were of animals that had never existed in England. And of the tools, one was of bone that had been carved by a steel knife. Like the fate of Peking man's remains, here was a mystery that would probably never be solved.

That winter Teilhard worked on an essay, "The Singularities of the Human Species," as an answer to the scientists who claimed that the difference between man and ape was one of degree only. Man was a cleverer animal perhaps, they said, but, biologically, an animal nonetheless. Teilhard argued that, although there had been no notable physical change, man had definitely crossed that boundary from the biosphere to the noosphere, from the animal world to the world of reflective thought. The Australopithecines were certainly simians, but simians with small canines who stood upright, he said, and the Pithecanthropines, Java man and Peking man, were certainly men, but men with the long, flattened skull of the ape.

In February a letter came from the Father General at Rome, giving Teilhard permission to spend three months in France. Perhaps, Teilhard thought, this might be the start of a precedent for a return every year. It could even be made in connection with his scientific work for the Wenner-Gren Foundation. Many of his old friends would be missing, and he looked forward more than ever to being with the few who remained. Augustin Valensin had died at the end of December. "It was he who taught me to think," Teilhard said. "It was a most beautiful death, calling on the sun and God at the same time," he wrote to his cousin Marguerite. "Then my other friend who first taught me to see the truth, Pierre Charles, has also gone: he too must have ended with simplicity and style. So I repeat the prayer that has become *my* prayer, 'May the Lord grant me, not for my own sake but for the sake of the cause I defend (the cause of the "most Great Christ") *to end well.*' "

Father Teilhard had become too well known to enjoy a quiet, peaceful return to his native France. When he arrived in Paris on June 9th, he found himself caught up in the same heavy schedule of meetings and receiving visitors, but now he felt the strain more than ever before. He gave a lecture on "Africa and Human Origins" and another on instinct in animals, both strictly scientific subjects, but everything he said was given so much space in the newspapers the publicity again became embarrassing to him. He learned that there were some, antagonistic to his views, who criticized him for coming back to France and had started a campaign against him. Though this hurt him deeply, Teilhard had nothing to say against his critics. "If you met the devil, I'd expect you to say, 'You know, he's not as bad as all that,' " his friend Pierre Leroy once said to him.

After four weeks in Paris Teilhard left with Leroy for a drive into the French countryside, first to Lyons and then to the famous Lascaux cave, discovered in 1940. At Lyons Teilhard was warmly welcomed by his Provincial Superior, who proved to be sympathetic and comforting. The whole place had a friendly atmosphere that brought peace after the hectic days in Paris. The rector and professors of the scholasticate where the two priests were lodged were cordial, and many of the students came to him, eager to know more about his philosophy. He was to look upon this visit as one of the bright spots of his stay in France.

On the way to Lascaux Teilhard wanted to stop off at Sarcenat, to see his old home once more. He went into the house alone while Leroy waited outside. The pastel portrait of him as a child still hung on the wall of the room where he was born, and his first collection of rocks, carefully labeled, was under the same glass case. He then strolled over the grounds and to the old church at Orcines where his parents and eight of his brothers and sisters were buried. "I shall never see Sarcenat again," Teilhard remarked to Leroy when they drove away.

The other bright spot of this visit to France was Lascaux. The war had been going on a year when some schoolboys, trying to rescue their dog, who had fallen into a crack of the earth, came upon this cave and were frightened by what they saw. For hundreds of feet, along the main cave and the corridors opening onto it, the walls were covered with brightly colored paintings of horses, deer, and bison, made some ten thousand years ago. They were so skillfully done that it is supposed that the artists were men taken out of the hunt to devote their full time to this work. This was Teilhard's first view of the cave, for in 1940, the year of its discovery, he was exiled in China by the war.

From Lascaux Teilhard returned to Paris, where, at the end of July he received word from Rome that his latest article could not be published, and furthermore it was suggested that he return to the United States. This meant cutting short his visit by almost a month. Those who saw him during his last few days in Paris, and in England where he made a short visit, noticed a haunting look of sadness beneath a cheerful, sometimes gay exterior.

"Pray for me that I may stand firm to the end," he said to a friend, and again to another, "Pray that I may not die embittered." Many times he repeated this prayer that he might end well. Five months after leaving France he wrote to his old friend Breuil: "The shadows are growing longer —and thicker—around us. My one great prayer (and I include in it all whom I love) is to 'end well.' One way or another I mean my death to seal that for which I have always lived."

He thought of his many writings known in manuscript form only and decided to try once again to express his ideas in such a way that the critics would find no fault with them. "Lord, grant that I may see, that I may see you, that I may see and feel you present in all things," he wrote in Latin, and in French he added: "Oh golden glow! Help me to the right action, the right word, help me to give the example that will reveal you best—without scandalizing, without rupture—through convergence."

When it was said that the twentieth century was not a religious one, he objected. "It is probably more religious than any other," he said. "How could it fail to be with such vast horizons and with such problems to be solved? The only thing that it has not yet is the God it can adore."

He finished his last great work in March 1955, an essay called "The Christique." "It is a long time since, in *Mass on the Altar of the World* and *The Divine Milieu,* I tried, in the light of my still half-formed vision of the world, to find the exact expression for my wonder and amazement. Today, after forty years of continual reflection, it is still the same fundamental view that I feel I must put forward, and share with others, but in its mature form—just once more. I must do so, I fear, with less freshness and exuberance of expression than I could command when I first came to it. But I still retain the same sense of wonder and of passion."

The Sorbonne planned a conference on paleontology in April of that year, and Father Teilhard was asked to participate in it. There were times when he longed to be in France again. "If only I could go back for an hour," he was heard to say. But a friendly letter came from his Provincial Superior warning him not to apply to Rome for permission at that time. Teilhard had to content himself with sending a paper to be read at the conference, with a note enclosed apologizing for his absence. Two days before the conference met, Father Teilhard died suddenly of a heart attack.

It was on Easter, always a favorite day for him, April 10, 1955. "When I die I should like it to be on the day of Resurrection," he had remarked the year before during a dinner at the French Consulate. The day was a splendid one, sunny and mild, with the trees in Central Park taking on their spring colors. Father Teilhard attended High Mass at St. Patrick's Cathedral, then took a walk through the park. In the afternoon, after attending a concert, he called on friends for tea. While there he suffered a heart attack, and at six o'clock the end came, suddenly and gently.

A simple funeral service was held at the chapel of the Jesuit House on Park Avenue. From there he was taken to the cemetery of the Jesuit novitiate at Saint Andrew-on-the-Hudson. Only Pierre Leroy, who was in the United States at the time, accompanied him on the ninety-mile journey that gray, rainy Tuesday. Father Teilhard's own words, from "Le Coeur de la Matier" came to the minds of many who knew him.

"Lord, since with every instinct of my being and through all the changing fortunes of my life, it is You whom I have ever sought, You whom I have set at the heart of universal matter, it will be in a resplendence which shines through all things and in which all things are ablaze, that I shall have the felicity of closing my eyes."

Epilogue

IN THE SPRING of 1965 a Mass was held at Saint Ignace's Church in Paris on the tenth anniversary of the death of Pierre Teilhard de Chardin.

"Ten years have passed since that day in April when the news of Pierre Teilhard de Chardin's death flashed over the wires from New York," said the priest, Father André Ravier. "We are gathered here tonight as a community of souls transcending all vain dispute, and bound in fidelity to a marvelous friendship. And we, his friends, still feel the sorrow we felt on that day. We feel it in our hearts and in our lives, for it is a wound that does not heal with time."

Among his listeners were fellow Jesuits who had defended Father Teilhard's beliefs and had stood by him in times of despair; scientists who had worked with him in the field and laboratory; nuns who had cared for him during an earlier illness; middle-aged men who, in youth, had been inspired by him in classrooms and lecture halls. There were relatives, but few were left now—one brother, nephews, nieces, and cousins. And some were there who had not known him in life, but were discovering him through his writings.

In his last paper, "Research, Work and Worship," Father Teilhard again stressed the need for the Church to keep up with the latest developments of knowledge instead of clinging to a limited understanding, several hundred years old, of the universe. The article was written in March 1955, exactly fifty-four years after he had taken his first simple vows as a Jesuit.

" 'Go quietly ahead with your scientific work without getting involved in philosophy and theology.' Throughout my whole life that is the advice (and the warning) that authority will be found repeatedly to have given me," he wrote.

"And such, too, I imagine [is] the directive given to many brilliant youngsters who are now, when the time is so opportune, entering the field of research.

"Such, too, the attitude of which, with all respect and yet with the assurance I draw from fifty years spent living in the heart of the problem, I should like to remark to those it properly concerns that it is psychologically un-viable and, what is more, directly opposed to the greater glory of God."

Death released Father Teilhard from his vows of obedi-ence to his Order's decision that he should not publish his books. A committee was formed of outstanding scholars from Europe and America to bring out all his unpublished works. At the time the Mass for him was held at Saint Ignace's Church, twelve of the well-thumbed manuscripts, once handed from friend to friend, were available in book form, and others were soon to follow.

"As his works are read, Father Teilhard is better known for the person he really was," Father Ravier continued. "But are we, his friends, wholly satisfied? Have our expectations been fulfilled? Here, tonight, those who knew him well, those who loved him, recall a Teilhard bearing little resemblance to the person now becoming known as the Teilhard of history. We know that the private person, the inner man, has not been 'grasped' by literature. Moreover, perhaps, he is ungraspable."

The list of Teilhard's published works continued to grow. There were editions of his essays and written lectures, of letters to relatives and friends, and even jottings from his notebooks. Translations of these books appeared in other countres, and as his fame spread, books about him appeared. Some were memoirs of scientific excursions taken with him, some were biographies, and some were discussions and explanations of his philosophy.

The Phenomenon of Man, the most important of Teilhard de Chardin's works, was published in Paris a few months after his death. Four years later, in 1959, the English translation appeared in London and New York. Teilhard began his preface with the statement: "If this book is to be properly understood, it must be read not as a work of metaphysics, still less as a theological essay, but purely and simply as a scientific treatise. The book deals with man *solely* as a phenomenon; but it also deals with the *whole* phenomenon of man."

In spite of this statement, and in spite of the fact that the introduction to the English translation was written, not by a theologian, but by the scientist and freethinker Sir Julian Huxley, it was obvious that this was not an ordinary scientific treatise. Teilhard traced the evolution of man starting with earth's formation, when there was only matter from which all life was formed, down to the present—and beyond, to that far distant goal toward which man has been climbing steadily.

"Up to now, has science ever troubled to look at the world other than from the *without?*" Teilhard asked. He wrote also of the *within* of things. He made no separation of the spiritual from the physical in man or the universe. Every element of the cosmos was positively woven with each of the others. "All around us, as far as the eye can see, the universe holds together, and only one way of considering it is really possible, that is, to take it as a whole, in one piece." In primordial matter there had been this global unity, and it has continued. "I repeat this same thing like a refrain on every rung of the ladder that leads to man; for if this is forgotten, nothing can be understood."

He expressed himself in a poetic, almost mystical style, which someone described as quite different from the "usual plonking style of the scientist." In his book were none of the technical phrases of the scientist or theologian, very few footnotes, and no references to sources of information from the works of others. He wrote from his own observations on a subject he knew well and felt intensely. When there was no word that expressed his exact meaning, he had a way of creating compound words, such as "noosphere," "cosmogenesis" and "Christogenesis," "hominization."

From the first publication of *The Phenomenon of Man* there had been the disputes and misunderstandings. A New York critic wrote of the controversy the book was sure to cause, and he added, "The thought and worthy discussion it will arouse would have been the author's dearest wish, and will be his greatest monument."

"Man came silently into the world," Father Teilhard had written in the chapter "The Birth of Thought." Man was born a direct lineal descendant of the whole process of life. When he reached the stage in his evolution to take that tremendous step across the threshold to thought and reflection, it was imperceptible. In appearance and in his way of life there was little to distinguish earliest man from the apes around him. This was a shocking thought to those who still clung to old, familiar dogmas. Father Teilhard was accused of ignoring the biblical story of creation, of failing to give importance to original sin and the fall of man, penitence, and redemption, which had been so much a part of Christianity for centuries.

These protests were answered by Catholics and non-Catholics in books, essays, lectures, and in letters written from one friend to another. A Protestant clergyman wrote that Teilhard de Chardin had given back to Christianity its true, religious meaning, of a universal, cosmic Christ. He had also freed the doctrine of Redemption from its narrow human interpretation. With a love on the scale of God, Christ's Redemption now embraced the totality of man and the universe.

Of his other major book, the Grand Rabbi of France declared, "Not for hundreds of years has there been so fine a book as *The Divine Milieu*." A Jesuit priest who had read the book expressed the thought many others later expressed, that here was a book written especially for him. It was as though someone quite unknown to him had searched for him and had written, with great force and sincerity, his own ideas and beliefs. A Canadian writer, in a letter to a friend, said of *The Phenomenon of Man*, "I've been devouring this shattering book. I've read it and reread it, and it's been a complete revelation, a great breath of fresh air blowing away the accumulation of dust and anachronisms; a great light suddenly illuminating the dark nave of a sleepy church."

While theologians, rejecting science, found fault with Father Teilhard's statements about man's beginning, scientists, rejecting religion, criticized him for his conclusions about man's future and his final goal. What could not be proven by experiment was not science, they said. Therefore Teilhard's works were not scientific. One of Teilhard's American colleagues described him as primarily a Christian mystic and secondly, although importantly, a scientist.

A British physiologist and Nobel prize-winner, Dr. Peter Medawar, was more hostile in his criticism. He ridiculed Teilhard's style of writing, called him a naturalist who practiced an intellectually unexacting kind of science, and accused him of deceiving himself, and in doing so, deceiving others. Immediately scientists from England, Scotland, France, and America came to Teilhard's defense. They agreed that while Teilhard's conclusions could not be proven through experiment, there was nothing in them contrary to scientific facts. "Unfortunately for Alfred Nobel and for biology," George Barbour wrote, "Teilhard's name will be remembered, even if constantly mispronounced, centuries after Dr. Medawar's lapse has been forgotten."

Julian Huxley wrote in his introduction to *The Phenomenon of Man* of the influence Teilhard was bound to have on the world's thinking. Through his wide scientific knowledge, combined with deep religious feeling and a strong sense of values, Teilhard would cause theologians to reconsider their ideas in the new perspective of scientific facts, and scientists to see the spiritual significance of their discoveries. Another scientist, the American Theodosius

Dobzhansky, wrote at the end of his book *Mankind Evolving*: "To modern man, so forlorn and spiritually embattled in this vast and ostensibly meaningless universe, Teilhard de Chardin's evolutionary idea comes as a ray of hope. It fits the requirements of our time."

When Teilhard, isolated in Peking, was working on *The Phenomenon of Man,* a philosophy of defeatism was fashionable among the intellectuals of Europe and America. Two world wars had been fought within a period of twenty-five years. Man seemed bent on destroying himself and his environment, it was said. There seemed no reason to try to go on. Father Teilhard did not share this attitude. It was unthinkable that man should end before he reached his final goal. Once and once only had the earth been able to envelop itself with life. Once and once only had life succeeded in crossing the threshold of reflection. Many millions of years had gone into this process and it was not likely to stop before its time unless the universe committed abortion, and that, Father Teilhard declared, was an absurd thought.

There was nothing shallow in his optimism, it was based on sound reasoning. He admitted that there were imperfections, of course, in a world still going through the stages of evolution. "Suffering and failure, tears and blood, so many by-products (often precious, moreover, and re-utilizable) begotten by the noosphere along the way." There had been so many failures for one success, so many days of misery for one hour of joy, so many sins for a solitary saint.

"After all, half a million years, perhaps a million, were required for life to pass from the pre-hominids to modern man. Should we now start wringing our hands because, less than two centuries after glimpsing a higher state, modern man is still at loggerheads with himself? Once again we have got things out of focus. To have understood the immensity around us, behind us, and in front of us, is already a first step. But if to this perception of depth another perception, that of *slowness,* be not added, we must realize that the transposition of values remains incomplete and that it can beget for our gaze nothing but an impossible world. Planetary movement involves planetary majesty. Would not humanity seem to us altogether static if, behind its history, there were not the endless stretch of its prehistory? Similarly, and despite an almost explosive acceleration of noogenesis at our level, we cannot expect to see the earth transform itself under our eyes in the space of a generation. Let us keep calm and take heart.

"In spite of all the evidence to the contrary, mankind may very well be advancing all round us at the moment— there are many signs whereby we can reasonably suppose that it is advancing. But if it is doing so, it must be—as is the way with very big things—doing so imperceptibly."

Bibliography

Books by Pierre Teilhard de Chardin

The Phenomenon of Man. New York: Harper & Row, 1959.

The Divine Milieu. New York: Harper & Row, 1960.

The Future of Man. New York: Harper & Row, 1964.

Hymn of the Universe. New York: Harper & Row, 1965.

Building the Earth. Wilkes-Barre, Pa.: Dimension Books, 1965.

The Appearance of Man. New York: Harper & Row, 1965.

Man's Place in Nature. New York: Harper & Row, 1966.

The Vision of the Past. New York: Harper & Row, 1966.

172   BIBLIOGRAPHY

Letters from a Traveler. New York: Harper & Row, 1962.

The Making of a Mind: Letters from a Soldier Priest: 1914–1919. New York: Harper & Row, 1965.

Letters from Egypt: 1905–1908. New York: Herder and Herder, 1965.

Letters from Paris: 1912–1914. New York: Herder and Herder, 1967.

Letters from Hastings. New York: Herder and Herder, 1968.

Letters to Two Friends: 1926–1952. New York: New American Library, 1968.

Letters to Léontine Zanta. New York: Harper & Row, 1969.

Correspondence: Pierre Teilhard de Chardin–Maurice Blondel. New York: Herder and Herder, 1967.

Books about Pierre Teilhard de Chardin

Barbour, George B. *In the Field with Teilhard de Chardin.* New York: Herder and Herder, 1965.

Cuénot, Claude. *Teilhard de Chardin: A Biographical Study.* Baltimore, Md.: Helicon Press, 1965.

Fülöp-Miller, René. *The Power and Secret of the Jesuits.* London: G. P. Putnam and Sons, 1930; paperback edition entitled *The Jesuits,* New York: Capricorn Books, 1963.

Kopp, Joseph V. *Teilhard de Chardin: A New Synthesis of Evolution.* New York: The Paulist Press, 1964.

Mooney, Christopher F. *Teilhard de Chardin and the Mystery of Christ.* New York: Harper & Row, 1966.

Mortier, Jeanne, and Marie-Louise Auboux (eds.). *The Teilhard de Chardin Album.* New York: Harper & Row, 1966.

Rabut, Olivier. *Teilhard de Chardin: A Critical Study.* New York: Sheed & Ward, 1961.

Raven, Charles E. *Teilhard de Chardin: Scientist and Seer.* New York: Harper & Row, 1962.

Rideau, Emile. *The Thought of Teilhard de Chardin.* New York: Harper & Row, 1967.

Speaight, Robert. *The Life of Teilhard de Chardin.* New York: Harper & Row, 1967.

de Terra, Helmut. *Memories of Teilhard de Chardin.* New York: Harper & Row, 1964.

Index